I0114226

Nation Iroquoise

THE IROQUOIANS AND THEIR WORLD

Editors

José António Brandão
Mary Druke Becker
William A. Starna

Nation Iroquoise

A SEVENTEENTH-CENTURY ETHNOGRAPHY OF THE IROQUOIS

Edited and with an introduction by
José António Brandão

Translated by
José António Brandão with K. Janet Ritch

UNIVERSITY OF NEBRASKA PRESS
LINCOLN AND LONDON

This book was published with the assistance of the Association for Canadian Studies in the United States and the Government of Canada.

Manufactured in the United States of America

Composition by Wilsted & Taylor Publishing Services

Library of Congress Cataloging-in-Publication Data

Nation iroquoise. English.
Nation Iroquoise : a seventeenth-century ethnography of the Iroquois / edited and with an introduction by José António Brandão ; [translated by José António Brandão with K. Janet Ritch].
p. cm.—(The Iroquoians and their world)
Text contains French transcription and English translation of original document with introduction in English.
". . . it seems unlikely that 'Nation Iroquoise' was written by someone other than René Cuillerier . . ."
Includes bibliographical references (p.) and index.
ISBN 0-8032-1323-9 (cloth : alk. paper)
1. Iroquois Indians—Social life and customs. 2. Iroquois Indians—History—17th century. 3. Iroquois Indians—Government relations. 4. Canada—History—To 1763 (New France) I. Brandão, José António, 1957– II. Cuillerier, René, 17th cent. III. Title. IV. Series.
E99.I7N3713 2003
974.7004'9755—dc21
2003050751

Contents

Preface

I found the document that is published here in translation for the first time in the National Archives of Canada in the late 1980s while doing research on Iroquois culture and on Iroquois-French relations. Titled "Nation Iroquoise," the document was a handwritten copy of an unsigned and undated French-language ethnography of the Iroquois left by someone who had been a captive among the Iroquois. The original document was housed in the Bibliothèque Mazarine in Paris and had lain buried there (as I later learned) since about 1789, and the transcript had been in Canada since it was made in 1931.[1] I learned that the document was unused, but not unknown. Father Lucien Campeau, historian of the Hurons and of the Jesuit missions in Canada, and W. J. Eccles, historian of New France, had both seen the document and had made transcripts of it decades earlier. Indeed, as early as 1900 Louis Bertrand, a chronicler of the Sulpician order of missionaries, noted its existence, and Waldo Leland listed it in his 1932 guide to materials related to American history housed in Paris.[2] Yet it appears that "Nation Iroquoise" remains little known and rarely cited, and the document's authorship is unresolved.[3] Needless to add, it has remained outside the research scope of students of the Iroquois who do not read French.

It seemed obvious to me that the information in "Nation Iroquoise" was valuable, and it informed my analysis of early Iroquois culture.[4] As a result of that work and of conversations about the document, scholars in a variety of disciplines expressed an interest in the document and wondered whether I could identify who wrote it and provide a translation for students of the Iroquois who did not read French. Already intrigued by the puzzle of the document's authorship, I needed little prodding to undertake the research to determine who might have written it. After all, if it can be established that the document is an original eyewitness account of Iroquois society in the seventeenth or eighteenth century, one can add it as an independent voice contributing to the body of material about the Iroquois.

I had completed my research on the document, the context of its creation, its authorship, and a draft translation when it was brought to my attention that other published versions of the document existed. Janet Ritch, who had agreed to look over my translation, learned from Lyse Roy and Alain Beaulieu about two publications dealing with the document. In 1996 Aurélien Boisvert published an edited and annotated version of "Nation Iroquoise" based on the Bibliothèque Mazarine manuscript. That same year Claude Gélinas and Roland Viau had planned to publish, along with other documents, a version of the document based on the copy in the National Archives of Canada. Disappointed by the quality of the editorial work in Boisvert's book, among other things, they went ahead with their plans.[5]

Despite these publications, I thought that my research could be a useful contribution to the extant literature. Although Boisvert and I arrived at a similar conclusion about authorship, my analysis of the document, the question of authorship, and its date of origin is more detailed than Boisvert's and is grounded in a wide range of historical sources. Boisvert devotes only four pages to these matters and provides no sources for the conclusions offered.[6] Gélinas and Viau did not seek to ascertain authorship and provided no editorial comment on the history of the document or regarding its contents. Viau, in a later work, attributed the document to a Jesuit priest whom Boisvert did not mention and who I contend could not have written the document.[7] None of these publications offered a translation of the document.

Yet another French transcription of the document is offered here because the extant printed versions are different from the manuscript document that serves as their sources. Gélinas and Viau's publication is based on a copy of the "original," and there are a number of differences (mostly in spelling variants and in lack of indication of deleted or added words) between the copy they used and the "original" in Paris. They also failed to indicate the "page breaks" in the document. Boisvert's *Nation Iroquoise* is based on the Paris document, but the published version is seriously altered: periods were added, new paragraphs and subject headings were created, spellings of Native groups were modernized, numbers were spelled out, and original page breaks were not indicated. In order for readers to make sense of the English translation, it seemed best to offer a version of the transcription that served as its basis. The transcription presented here adheres as closely as modern technology will allow to the version of "Nation Iroquoise" in the Bibliothèque Mazarine.

This work is divided into two parts. The first section offers a brief overview of Iroquois culture and of Iroquois-French relations in the period in which the document was most likely written. That is followed by an attempt to explain who might have written "Nation Iroquoise," and who could not have done so, and to explore the contribution of "Nation Iroquoise" to understanding the Iroquois and their culture. Part 2 is taken up by the transcription and translation of the document.

Acknowledgments

This is a small book whose creation has been quite drawn out. The major benefit of the extra time, aside from actually improving the work, has been the opportunity it has afforded me to accumulate ever greater debts of gratitude to friends and colleagues. (What sounded like pleas to "finish the damn thing" were, I am certain, offered to encourage me and were not signs that I had pestered them beyond endurance.) To Gary Dunham my deepest thanks for his continued encouragement of my work. His commitment to promoting scholarship in its myriad forms makes it a pleasure to be associated with him and the University of Nebraska Press. Thanks also to Jane Curran for her careful and thoughtful editing and commentary. Ronald Davis, former chair of the Department of History at Western Michigan University, and Elise Jorgens, former dean of the school's College of Arts and Sciences, provided a reduced teaching load that allowed time to research and write. Grants from the history department's Burnham-Macmillan Endowment supported a research trip to the National Archives of Canada to double-check research notes, the following up of new leads about "Nation Iroquoise" and its origins, and other minor research-related costs.

Monsieur Pierre Gasnault, *conservateur en chef* of the Bibliothèque Mazarine in Paris, kindly arranged to have a microfilm copy of "Nation Iroquoise" made and shared with me his knowledge of seventeenth-century French orthography. Father Lucien Campeau shared his understanding of "Nation Iroquoise" with me and encouraged my research efforts. Ramsay Cook, Conrad Heidenreich, and William A. Starna, long-suffering mentors and friends, read versions of the whole manuscript and provided valuable suggestions for improvement. Conrad, who along with Bill saved me from egregious errors of fact regarding fauna and flora, was kind enough to produce the map that accompanies the text. Portions of part I of the book were presented as "Nation Iroquoise: An Ethnography in Search of an Author" at the Annual Conference on Iroquois Research, Rensselaerville, New York, in October 1998. Thanks to the conference participants, especially James Axtell, Mary Druke-Becker, and Louise Johnston, for their helpful comments and suggestions. Thanks also to the anonymous reviewers at the University of Nebraska Press for their comments and suggestions for improvements.

Joseph L. Peyser provided invaluable help during the early stages of the translation. His insight and generosity of spirit are deeply appreciated. Janet Ritch took my original translation and improved upon it in ways that were, and are, beyond my ability. Without her expertise, keen critical eye, and patience this project could not have been completed. I am delighted that she agreed to accept publication credit for her contribution to the project. The errors that remain are, of course, *mea culpa, mea culpa, mea maxima culpa.*

Lastly, my thanks to Mary and Robert for the good grace and patience with which they accepted my absences as I closed my office door and slipped, yet again, into the past. This work is dedicated to Robert because he asked me to do so, and as we all know, any child who wants his name mentioned in a work of history deserves to have his wish fulfilled—not only because it is a small price to exact for fatherly absences, but also in the vain hope that he might one day read beyond this page and see why the past holds such fascination.

Part 1. Context

The Iroquois and Their French Neighbors

Hindsight has led some historians of French-Iroquois relations to posit that conflict between the two peoples was inevitable.[1] However, although the early history of contact between these two groups was turbulent, there were interludes of peace, and each group came to use and rely upon the other, even if they did not fully trust them.[2] There was nothing inevitable about any of this. Accommodation and warfare were the products of decisions (informed and otherwise) made by specific people, at given times, in response to particular circumstances and pressures, and often reflected the aspirations and cultural values of the Iroquois and French. The Iroquois were determined to protect their culture and their political integrity, and the French sought to secure their foothold in the New World and expand the reach of their economic and political empire in North America. Neither group was always able to see how cooperation could benefit its particular self-interest, and military solutions to political dilemmas were readily accepted by French and Iroquois alike. It was within this turbulent context that French-Iroquois relations were played out during the seventeenth century, and it was these unsettled conditions that led to the capture of the author of "Nation Iroquoise."

Iroquois Settlements around 1660

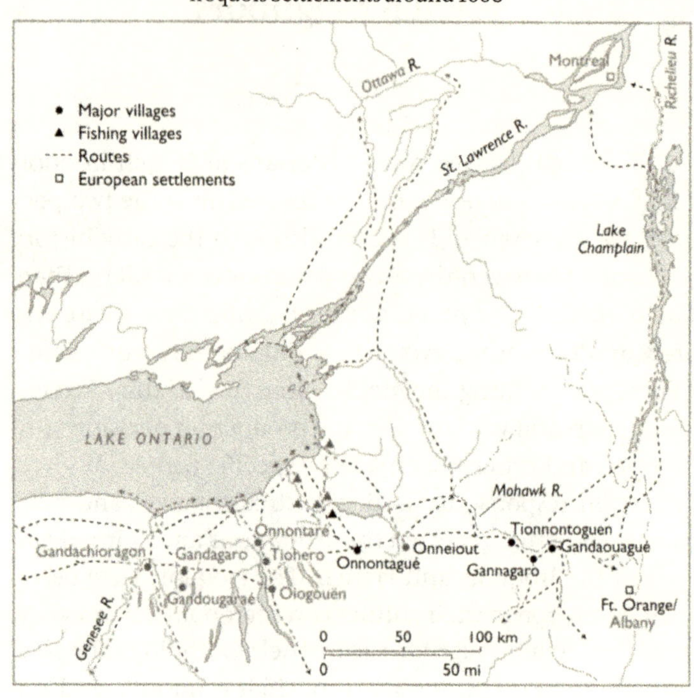

Ottawa R.
Montreal
Richelieu R.
Major villages
Fishing villages
Routes
European settlements
St. Lawrence R.
Lake Champlain
LAKE ONTARIO
Mohawk R.
Onnontaré
Tionnontoguen
Gandachiorágon
Gandagaro
Tiohero
Onnontagué
Onneiout
Gannagaro
Gandaouagué
Gandougaraé
Oiogouen
Genesee R.
Ft. Orange/
Albany
0
50
100 km
0
50 mi

When the French first met them, the people who came to be known as the Five Nations Iroquois (Senecas, Cayugas, Onondagas, Oneidas, and Mohawks) lived in an area south of Lake Ontario and bounded roughly by the Genesee River on the west and the Hudson on the east (see map). The Iroquois called themselves the *Hodenosaunee* ("People of the Longhouse"). Their traditions tell of their origins in what is now upstate New York, while the archaeological record suggests both in situ development and movement from a more southerly point of origin.[3] The five groups that made up the League of the Iroquois spoke different languages but shared a common culture. Some of the key features of that culture were the roles and status of women, the clan system, and the various functions of warfare.

The Iroquois were a matrilineal society wherein descent was traced through women. According to William N. Fenton, "Each village band, or community, is composed of one or more clan segments, or lineages. The lineage is a core of mothers, sisters, and daughters who, in native theory, are a longhouse family or residential group, together with a fringe of spouses of other lineages."[4] Men and women from the same lineages were not supposed to marry each other and had to seek spouses from outside family groups. Each nation among the Iroquois recognized at least three clans (Turtle, Wolf, and Bear), and the need to seek marriage partners outside of one's family served to create links and alliances with unrelated people within the village, among other villages of that nation (some nations had more than one village), and in the villages of other nations in the Iroquois League.[5]

The Iroquois were horticulturalists and hunters. Corn, squash, and beans were their staple crops. The three crops, known as the "Three Sisters," were planted together in small mounds in communal fields located outside the village palisades. The fields were cleared by the men, but crops were planted and tended by the women. The men, when not at war or engaged in diplomacy and trade, hunted and fished to augment the Iroquois diet. The Iroquois hunted almost anything (beaver, muskrat, squirrel) but preferred deer and a variety of wild fowl as staples. The men also fished with spears, nets, and weirs for a variety of fish and turtle species. Eels were particularly sought because they could be dried, smoked, and preserved for use during the winter months. This type of subsistence pattern meant that the Iroquois lived in semi-permanent villages (moving only once the resources of a given area had been exhausted) and also needed large tracts of land as hunting territories.[6] The latter included lands north of Lake Ontario and led them into conflict with other groups who also sought to exploit the region.

The matrilineal nature of Iroquois society, along with the significant role women had in providing basic group sustenance, gave women a good deal of power. Women could initiate warfare or seek to put an end to wars. Political or military deliberations often originated in women's councils.[7] Matters of enough import were then brought to the attention of male leaders. The latter (at least "civil" leaders) were often chosen by women, and it was from local village and tribal leaders that national leaders were chosen.[8]

The clan system was also intricately connected to warfare, which was another key aspect of Iroquois society. Warfare could be undertaken for a number of reasons including the desire to gain honor, to exact revenge, and to gain captives. The latter could be used in exchanges with other nations who had taken Iroquois captives, for torture or, of increasing importance as the seventeenth century wore on, to adopt into a clan to replace a clan member who had died of natural causes, of new epidemic diseases, or in war. As the number of Europeans grew in the areas surrounding the Iroquois, so did the frequency of epidemic diseases, the number of deaths, and the need to capture people to replace those lost. Up to 1669 the Iroquois captured from 1,434 to 1,568 people. From 1680 to 1700 they captured 2,384 to 2,608. This represents a 60 percent increase.[9]

According to French Jesuit Joseph Lafitau, the need to replace lost kin and to shore up clan lineages made war a "necessary exercise for the Iroquois."[10] Writing in the mid-1700s, English naturalist John Bartram observed: "Now their numbers being very much diminished . . . they very politically strive to Strengthen themselves not only by alliances with their neighbours, but . . . [by] prisoners they take; they are almost always accepted by the relations of a warrior slain. . . . This custom is as antient as our knowledge of them, but when their number of warriors was more than twice as many as now, the relations would more frequently refuse to adopt the prisoners but rather chuse to gratify their thirst of revenge."[11] Another factor that complicated Iroquois politics, and that also added pressure to take captives, was the presence of European nations who surrounded the Iroquois and limited their freedom to act as they had or as they wished. As diseases led to depopulation and reduced the pool of males from which the Iroquois could draw warriors, more captives were needed to bolster the size of the armies that the Iroquois needed in order to contend with Europeans.[12]

The Europeans nearest to the Iroquois, the Dutch, were not much of a threat. The Dutch population was small and remained confined to a few tiny fortified positions at the eastern most fringe of Iroquois territory. The Dutch also needed the Iroquois to trap furs, which were taken in exchange for European wares including, by 1640, guns.[13] The Iroquois added these weapons to their existing arsenal in their exercise of warfare against a variety of Native foes. The French, on the other hand, proved more problematic. At first they settled far from Iroquoia toward the mouth of the St. Lawrence River, but despite their small population, they expanded quickly and came to pose a threat to the Iroquois.

The first French explorers in North America came in search of riches and of the water passage to the East that had eluded Christopher Columbus in the late 1400s. No such passage existed, but it took decades to determine that, and by then the French had settlements in North America and were set on finding a convenient route across the continent to the Pacific Ocean.[14] The society that developed in New France came to value military ability and held notions about status and rank that often led them to make the sort of decision that, by today's standards, might appear economically irrational.[15] The precarious position of the French in North America, surrounded by Indians and more populous European neighbors, only strengthened the role of the military in the colony.[16]

Although the French never did find vast deposits of gold, as had Spanish explorers, their early voyages led to what would become an important trade in beaver furs, which could be used to make hats in France, and which were in inadequate supply in Europe to meet the demand. The key to expanding that trade, given the small French population, was to trade with Native nations who had easy access to hunting territories and to make alliances to trade with them. Westward exploration, coincidently, was also linked to alliances with Native nations who knew the interior of the continent and who could show the French the way and protect them in their travels.[17]

It very soon became evident to the French that access to the interior and to the tribes who lived there was conditional on control of the St. Lawrence River. It was the main passage to the interior and all that lay there. Unfortunately for the French, and for the Iroquois as well, the tribes along the St. Lawrence and lower Great Lakes were those with whom the Iroquois were at war. The groups in question, especially the Hurons and Algonquins, took the opportunity to use French need to fulfill their own plans. If the French wanted help, then they would have to help their new allies against those who harassed them. Thus in 1609, 1610, and 1615 Samuel de Champlain, who governed the French colony, sided with the Hurons and Algonquins against their Iroquois foes.

Despite this rocky start, both Champlain and some Iroquois were prepared to try to negotiate peace.[18] In 1626 a short-lived truce was negotiated, and in 1641 the Mohawk Iroquois tried to arrange peace. In 1645 the French sought to broker a peace with the Iroquois. Each time the Iroquois entered negotiations with the apparent aim of neutralizing French influence so that they could attack the Hurons and Algonquins unfettered by French support.[19] But in 1645 the French refused to abandon their allies. They did not trust the Iroquois and needed their Great Lakes allies to secure their hold on the fur trade and on the West. This rejection of the Iroquois peace offer, in addition to the building of French settlements in areas the Iroquois claimed as their own and as their hunting lands, led to a major outbreak of war. Between 1645 and 1653, when the Iroquois—this time the Onondagas—tried to arrange a truce, the French were attacked thirty-four times and had forty-seven people captured or killed.[20]

The reasons for extending the olive branch of peace in 1653 appear to have been many. Some Iroquois feared a major reprisal from the massed remnants of those people whom they had already dislocated. Others may have wanted a respite from war to consolidate their gains, and still others seemed to have been trying to lull the French into complacency in order to lure from their midst those Hurons whom the Iroquois wanted to incorporate into their villages and who had sought refuge among the French.[21] Whatever the Iroquois reasons, the French leapt at the opportunity that the Iroquois presented to end hostilities. In return for agreeing to peace, the French demanded access to Iroquois villages so that Jesuit missionaries could try to convert them. The French reasoned that Catholic Iroquois would not go to war against those who instilled in them these new values.

Unfortunately for the French, the situation changed. The Iroquois' fear of reprisal quickly passed, and the Jesuit presence proved too disruptive. By 1658 raiding against the French was again a regular occurrence. Between that date and the end of 1661, the Iroquois launched twenty-two raids against the French and removed ninety-one people from the colony—sixty-two as captives and twenty-nine killed.[22] On 25 October 1661 the author of "Nation Iroquoise" became another casualty in the ongoing conflict between the Iroquois and the French.

Nation Iroquoise and Its Authorship

Determining the authorship of an unsigned handwritten document can be a relatively uncomplicated process if one has a clear notion of when it was penned and who might have written the document, and if one can compare the material in question with known letters and other documents left by that person. That, unfortunately, is not the case with "Nation Iroquoise." It is undated and could have been written by any of a large number of people of whom few, if any, left posterity any writing samples. Moreover, the version of "Nation Iroquoise" left behind is likely a copy of the original made at a later date, and handwriting comparisons would not be possible even if a likely candidate for authorship was clearly identified. Ascertaining authorship, then, requires a careful study of the document's history and the document itself for clues and a wide-ranging discussion that attempts to ascertain who could and who could not have written it.

The document in question has a cover with the title of "Nation Iroquoise" written upon it. However, the title at the top of the first numbered folio of text translates as "Abridgement of the Lives and Customs and Other Particulars of the Iroquois Nation which is divided into Five Villages, namely Agnez, Onney8t, Nontagué, Goyog8an, and Sonnont8ans."[1] This small document (175 × 115 mm, or 7 × 4.5 inches) was originally housed in the Séminaire de Saint-Sulpice in Paris and came to the Bibliothèque Mazarine during the French Revolution.[2] A copy was made for the Canadian Archives in August 1931 by a Madame Joubert.[3] The "original" consists of thirty folios of text and a cover sheet all stitched together to form a small booklet. There is writing on both sides of each unlined sheet of paper, but only the recto (right side) of each folio is numbered on the upper-right-hand side. The numbers on the upper recto side of the folios appear to be slightly different from those in the text, but this may be more apparent than real since the numbers used to mark the folios are very small and thicker.[4] The smallness of the numbers, and the greater care needed to make the small numbers needed to fit into the little space available on the upper right of each folio, may account for the minor difference.

The writing on the cover sheet, however, clearly appears to be in a different hand from that in the rest of the document. The differences are most noticeable in the letters *N* and *r*. It is almost certain that the cover was added sometime after the text was written. The latter contention is supported by the fact that Iroquois is spelled "Iroquoise" on the cover and is consistently spelled "Irokoise" throughout the text of the document. The latter is a common seventeenth-century spelling, and the former is the usual spelling in the eighteenth century. Indeed, the cover sheet may have been added at the Bibliothèque Mazarine. The first folio of text carries the accession stamps of both the Séminaire de Saint-Sulpice and the Bibliothèque Mazarine, but the cover sheet, "Nation Iroquoise," is stamped twice and only with the Bibliothèque Mazarine stamp.

The writing in "Nation Iroquoise" is small, neat, and in evenly spaced lines. It looks like a "clean" copy of a written *mémoire* or verbal report. There are a few instances of words crossed out and, in one or two places, an omitted word added in the margin or letters added above the original word. As well, although there are clearly set-off paragraphs, there are few sentences punctuated with commas or periods. Overall, however, it looks like a rewritten version of a report. Indeed, internal evidence suggests that the document in question was written in the late seventeenth or early eighteenth century. In addition to spelling and grammar common to the early 1600s there is a scattering of spelling adopted only in the 1700s (e.g., *nôtre* rather than *nostre,* and *être* rather than *estre*).[5] The only reasonable explanation for such a mixture is that someone made a copy of an early document and, either deliberately or inadvertently, inserted the spelling of a later period.[6]

"Nation Iroquoise" is divided into ten unequal sections, each with a title written in large letters. Each section of the document deals with some aspect of Iroquois life or culture. "Nation Iroquoise" begins with a general geographic and topographic introduction to Iroquoia followed by sections on religion, types and processes of councils, councils concerning war, private war councils, mourning councils, Iroquois nature, Iroquois qualities, Iroquois superstitions, and Iroquois mourning rituals. In most sections the author both describes Iroquois culture and adds his personal interpretation and feelings about what he witnessed.

Although the document is unsigned and undated, it is not without clues about the identity of the author and about when "Nation Iroquoise" may have been originally written.[7] The author is clearly male. This is evident from the tone of his descriptions of female roles and activities. There is both a sense of novelty and detachment in his characterization of women's roles that is missing from his descriptions of councils and warfare. He does, however, seem to be aware of the wide variety of women's work and responsibilities. He calls the fort at what came to be Albany, New York, "Orange" (f. 1r). The author speaks well of the "*Reverend pères Jesuites*" and of their efforts to convert the Iroquois (ff. 3r–3v), and he refers to their authority on one occasion to support one of his observations (f. 10r). He mentions the Iroquois conquest of villages of over 1,500 people and the widespread use of guns (f. 7r, f. 8r), and he reveals that he was captured by the Iroquois and adopted into one of their clans (f. 14v). He appears to have been a captive for some time, apparently passed a winter among them, and proved himself a trustworthy member of the clan. Once he traveled alone with a pregnant woman of his adopted clan to meet her husband on the latter's return from hunting (f. 14v). This contact with women probably explains how he became familiar with the various roles of Iroquois women. The author does not clearly identify which tribe captured and adopted him, but because only the Oneidas are mentioned by name in the document (f. 7v, f. 12r), it seems reasonable, although not certain, to suggest that his time was spent among them. During the period of his captivity he saw more than eight men, both French and Native, tortured and killed (f. 7v). Finally, it is clear that the author related his observations at the request of another person (f. 3r). This unidentified "Monsieur" is addressed several times in the course of the document.

All this suggests a time frame after 1656 for the document's creation. By then gun use was fairly widespread among the Iroquois, and the Jesuits had attempted to build missionary outposts in Five Nations' villages. As well, by 1656 the Iroquois had concluded several large-scale wars against Natives in the Great Lakes region, the best-known of these being the war against the Hurons in the late 1640s. However, it is harder to be more precise. The reference to Iroquois contact with the Jesuits, for example, could have referred to Father Jogues's work among the Mohawks during his captivity in the 1640s. Calling Albany "Orange" could be taken to mean that the Dutch had yet to lose control of the area to the English, and that would provide a terminal date in the mid-1660s or early 1670s—depending on when the French decided to date the Dutch loss of their colony to the English. Unfortunately, the French referred to Albany as Orange until 1763. The reference to conquered villages is also of limited value in trying to establish a more precise time frame. The villages taken by the Iroquois might have been those of the Hurons attacked in the 1640s or those of the Illinois destroyed in the wars of the 1680s. The author's observation of French and Indians being tortured before his eyes is somewhat more helpful. Iroquois warfare against the French reached its peak in the seventeenth century, and the years 1650 to 1655, 1658 to 1662, and 1687 to 1697 were periods of particularly intense warfare against the French.[8] Iroquois warfare, including raids against the French, continued into the eighteenth century, but by then the Iroquois did not torture their French prisoners as readily. The fact that the author was an Iroquois captive helps narrow the time frame to a degree, but hundreds of people were captured by the Iroquois after 1650, and scholars know the details of the lives of very few and know little more than the names of most others.[9]

In short, although these clues narrow the limits of the search for authorship, identifying the author with certainty seems a remote possibility. Even if a likely individual could be found, and samples of his handwriting were extant, a comparative handwriting analysis could not be used to confirm authorship because "Nation Iroquoise" is a scribe's handiwork. The best that can be hoped for is to make a persuasive case for an individual after eliminating as many potential candidates as possible.

Since most of the evidence pointed to the latter half of the seventeenth century—however indecisively—it seemed best to start there. Research in seventeenth-century French archival material had turned up no other copies of "Nation Iroquoise," nor any other material that might have served as a basis for it. My recollection of published primary sources on Iroquois culture did not suggest any documents identical to "Nation Iroquoise," but a more methodical search seemed in order to confirm that "Nation Iroquoise" was not a copy of something that had already been published or that it had not been "cribbed" from some other source, since published.

The Jesuits' writings seemed to be a logical place to start because some Jesuits had been captured by the Iroquois, and because they were prolific writers and tried to understand cultures and how they functioned. The Jesuits wrote at the request of their superior in Quebec and often addressed themselves to that person in their letters and reports. Moreover, almost all their correspondence related to Canada has been published (the rest is in the process of being published), and the author spoke well of the Jesuits. However, nothing in the various collections of the Jesuits' writings matched "Nation Iroquoise."[10]

Was it possible that one of the priests wrote the document and that it had, for some reason, remained unpublished and had been lost to the order?[11] A survey of the Jesuits who might fit the author profile taken from the document and who might have written "Nation Iroquoise" pointed to Father Pierre Millet as a likely candidate. He was a missionary to the Oneidas, was captured by the Iroquois in 1689, and was adopted into an Oneida clan.[12] A check of the Jesuit *Relations* for his correspondence revealed a letter written from Oneida in 1674 in which he provided an analysis of Iroquois clans and of how councils were convened.[13] However, it is a decidedly shorter discussion of these matters than the one in "Nation Iroquoise." It is, of course, possible that he wrote "Nation Iroquoise" after 1674. The author of that document mentioned that he was adopted by the Oneidas, and Father Millet was not adopted until 1689. Regretfully though, at least in terms of shortening the search, one must rule out Father Millet as the author of "Nation Iroquoise." It is hard to fathom why he would return to the subject of Iroquois culture and councils after his 1674 report. By that date the *Relations* were no longer being published annually, and the Jesuits knew Iroquois culture well enough for the purposes of their work among them. Even had he written "Nation Iroquoise" later, it is hard to account for its presence among the papers of the Sulpicians without a copy in Jesuit hands. The two orders sought to avoid conflict, but they were not always on the best of terms—especially after the Sulpicians began their own missions to the Iroquois in 1668.[14] More telling as a reason to eliminate Father Millet from consideration are the references to the Jesuits. It is extremely unlikely that a Jesuit would refer to the Society of Jesuits in the third person. He would not write that the "*Reverend pères Jesuites*" worked among the Iroquois. Rather he would state that *nos pères* (our fathers) worked among the Iroquois.[15]

After this elimination of the Jesuits as potential authors, and since the document was found in a Sulpician house, it seemed best to turn to the rather short list of published Sulpician accounts of exploration and contact with Indians. But nothing in the writings of Dollier de Casson, Bréhant de Galinée, and François de Belmont bore any resemblance to "Nation Iroquoise."[16] Nor did a check of the various collections of Sulpician writings and correspondence turn up anything.[17] As previously noted, A. L. Bertrand knew of the existence of "Nation Iroquoise" in 1900 and thought that possibly one of the Sulpician priests who had served in

Canada might have been its author.[18] Unfortunately the document is not mentioned in official correspondence. Monsieur Louis Tronson, the superior of the Sulpicians, asked priests for details of events from their respective missions and acknowledged material sent to him, but nothing fitting the description of "Nation Iroquoise" is mentioned in letters to or from him.[19] Moreover, since not one of the Sulpician missionaries who served in New France fits the author profile in "Nation Iroquoise," one must reluctantly conclude that it was not written by a Sulpician and that it came into their possession through someone else.[20]

A search through the works of other seventeenth-century French chroniclers and observers such as Chevalier de Baugy, Pierre Boucher, Marie de l'Incarnation, Joseph Lafitau, Baron Lahontan, Claude-Charles de La Potherie, Nicholas Perrot, Pierre Radisson, and Gabriel Sagard proved equally fruitless.[21] Nor did a search through a variety of edited collections of primarily seventeenth-century documents and anonymous *mémoires* turn up a comparable account.[22]

However, the mystery of who wrote "Nation Iroquoise" appears to be on its way to resolution when it is compared to *Relation par lettres de l'Amerique septentrionale*.[23] Originally credited to the Jesuit Antoine Silvy, the work is now widely recognized as having come from the quill of Antoine-Denis Raudot, *intendant* of New France from 1705 to 1710. Portions of the sections on the Iroquois in this book are identical to "Nation Iroquoise."[24] Raudot changed the order of the subjects dealt with in "Nation Iroquoise," shortened some passages, and often changed a word or expression, but overall there is little doubt that he copied much of the material on the Iroquois in his *Relation* from "Nation Iroquoise."[25] One or two examples should suffice to make the case.[26]

According to Raudot, "Celuy qui a quelque proposition à faire ou quelque nouvelle à dire commence par assembler les anciens de sa famille, et si c'est quelque chose qui regarde les guerriers, on fait entrer un capitaine ou deux de cette même famille pour estre temoin de ce qui est proposé."[27] The author of "Nation Iroquoise" explained the process in these terms: "Celuy donc ou celle qui a quelques propositions a faire com̃ence par assembler les anciens de sa famille et si c'est quelque chose qui regarde les guerriers on fait venir un ou deux capitaines de cette même famille pour être témoins de la chose qu'on propose."[28] Regarding Iroquois religion, Raudot wrote that "ces sauvages Iroquois adorent le soleil, et c'est à luy qu'ils s'adressent tant pour la chasse que pour la guerre; ils n'entreprennent jamais rien sans avoir donné auparavant à fumer à cet astre."[29] The author of "Nation Iroquoise" remarked that "la religion de ces peuples consiste en bien peu de chose ils recoñoissent point d'autre Dieu que le Soleil et c'est a luy qui ils s'adressent dans toutes leurs nécessités tant pour la guerre que pour la chasse c'est pourquoy ils n'entrepreñent jamais rien sans auoir doñe auparauant à fumer a cet astre."[30] The last example is most telling because of the ambiguous and unique phrasing of the sentence alluding to sun worship.

This, of course, does not answer the question of who wrote "Nation Iroquoise"; it is clear that it was not Raudot.

Antoine-Denis Raudot was not captured by the Iroquois and never lived among them.[31] Yet, he obviously copied and condensed portions of "Nation Iroquoise" for his book. Did he know the author of "Nation Iroquoise"? If not, how had he obtained a copy of it? Was Raudot the anonymous "Monsieur" mentioned in the document? Was it he who had asked the original author to put quill to paper regarding his experiences among the Iroquois? Or is the copy now in the Bibliothèque Mazarine one that was copied from the original for Raudot to use as he had used the works of others? Indeed, was "Nation Iroquoise" the lost *mémoire* of Louis La Porte de Louvigny that Raudot was said to have used as the basis for part of his manuscript?

The history of Raudot's *Relation* is somewhat complex and is worth a closer look. When Father Camille de Rochemonteix discovered the manuscript of what came to be known as Raudot's *Relation* in the Royal Library of Berlin in the late 1800s, he thought it was the work of the Jesuit Father Antoine Silvy, who had served as a missionary in New France in the latter part of the seventeenth century. Rochemonteix was convinced that the Jesuit historian Pierre-François-Xavier Charlevoix had used "Silvy's" document while writing his multivolume history of New France and that the manuscript of the *Relation* was deposited at the College of Louis-le-Grand in 1761 along with Charlevoix's other papers.[32] The manuscript of the *Relation* was certainly there in the 1760s. The *Relation* was catalogued in 1764 before the college's papers were sold off, but when it arrived is uncertain.[33] What Rochemonteix, apparently, never learned is that the copy he found was not the only one extant. Sometime in the early twentieth century yet another Jesuit, Father Jean Delanglez, found what was clearly the rough draft of Raudot's manuscript among the official papers of French colonial officials.[34] It comprised one entire volume in the series of volumes, housed in the Archives Nationales in Paris, which dealt primarily with the correspondence of New France's leading government officials.[35] Misleadingly titled "Sioux ou Nadouesis," the first part of the volume contains "chapters" in the form of "letters" and is similar in content and style to the published version of the *Relation*. Included as well are copies of some of the documents that form the basis of the letters' contents. (None match "Nation Iroquoise.") There is also a great deal of crossed out material and commentary in the margins in a variety of different writing styles. At folio 98 the title "Memoire sur l'amerique septentrionalle" appears for the first time. At folio 260 the title changes to "Suitte de la relation par lettres de l'Amerique septentrionalle." Thereafter, letters 44 to 89 of the document are the same as those in the manuscript document Rochemontiex published. The Archives Nationales version has one extra letter.

Equally as important as the discovery of the early draft of the *Relation* is the fact that nineteenth-century French archivist Pierre Margry had noted that the document in question was written by Antoine Raudot and was based upon a *mémoire* of Louis La Porte de Louvigny. Louvigny was a captain in the colonial regular troops and went on to be named governor of Three-Rivers.[36] Margry referred future researchers to a letter of 24 September 1709 as proof of his assertion regarding Louvigny's part in the document's creation. Margry did not, however, indicate who had written the letter or where it could be found, but the context of the statement suggested that the letter was written by either Raudot or Louvigny.[37] In 1939 Delanglez credited the *Relation*, based on Margry's note, to Raudot, and in 1940 Vernon Kinietz, also based on Margry's note, attributed the *Relation* to Raudot. Kinietz further added that, regardless of Louvigny's contribution, part of Raudot's *Relation* was based on the memoirs of Pierre-Charles de Liette.[38] De Liette was a captain in the French colonial army who served with Henri de Tonty in the *pays d'en haut*. De Liette's *mémoire* is well known, but no one has found that of Louvigny.[39] Could "Nation Iroquoise" be it?

Unfortunately, tempting as it is to try to resolve two mysteries in one fell swoop, "Nation Iroquoise" is not Louvigny's lost *mémoire*. There is little reason to question, if anyone still does, that Raudot wrote the *Relation* that has come to be attributed to him. A comparison of his handwriting in signed letters with that in the draft version of his manuscript removes all doubt. It is also clear that Margry was correct in concluding that Raudot based his work on material from Louvigny. In a short note, at the end of a long narrative account of his travels in New France in the fall of 1709, Raudot informed Minister of the Marine Pontchartrain, who was responsible for New France, that he was sending him a relation about Canada based upon a *mémoire* by Louvigny who, he observed, "knows perfectly well the nations" of Canada.[40] Raudot was, of course, correct about the extent of Louvigny's knowledge about New

France's Native allies, and others shared Raudot's assessment of Louvigny's capacity in this area.[41] And Louvigny was well regarded by the Iroquois. For example, in 1699, at a time when the French had been pressuring the Iroquois to conclude a firm peace with them, Louvigny, *commandant* at Fort Frontenac, was charged with contravening the king's prohibition against trading at the post and arrested in early 1700.[42] One of the conditions for peace eventually demanded by the Iroquois was that Louvigny be released and returned to Fort Frontenac.[43]

Yet, regardless of his apparent importance as a source for Raudot's *Relation*, Louvigny does not fit the author's profile provided in "Nation Iroquoise." Most of Louvigny's time was spent among the tribes in the *pays d'en haut* and not among the Iroquois.[44] Indeed, in 1720, in recognition of his importance in the Upper Great Lakes region, Louvigny was named *commandant des pays d'en haut*.[45] And although he fought against the Iroquois several times, he was never a captive among them, never wintered among them, and was never adopted by the Iroquois into one of their clans.[46] His most prolonged stay near the Iroquois was during the winter of 1699–1700 while he was *commandant* at Fort Frontenac. In an account of his actions during that winter, made in defense of charges that he had traded illegally, Louvigny made no mention of ever leaving the fort.[47] Nor would he have had to downplay such visits had they taken place, since part of his mission was to do everything in his power to keep the Iroquois engaged in the peace process begun in 1699. Indeed, his defense against the charges of trading was that he had accepted furs as gifts from the Iroquois during a number of meetings aimed at furthering peace talks.[48]

In the end, one must conclude that "Nation Iroquoise" is another in an apparently growing list of sources from which Raudot plagiarized his now famous book. At the very least Raudot's reliance on "Nation Iroquoise" for his sections on the Iroquois resolved one important question: "Nation Iroquoise" was written sometime before Raudot completed his manuscript in 1709. Raudot's use of the document is telling in another important way: it suggests that the author of "Nation Iroquoise," or his adventure, was known. To think otherwise is to beg the question of how "Nation Iroquoise" came to be written or how Raudot or Louvigny got their hands on it. (One must concede the possibility that it was Louvigny who brought the document to Raudot's attention.)

After one refines the time frame of the document's creation somewhat and eliminates a significant number of potential authors, the problem of precisely who wrote "Nation Iroquoise" and when is somewhat nearer to resolution. It can now be said that "Nation Iroquoise" was written before 1709, probably by someone who was captured and adopted by the Oneidas, who was taken into their confidence, who wintered among them, whose story was known to people, and who may have had some connection to the Sulpicians since the document was preserved by them. If that does not exactly pinpoint a time, place, and person, it does indicate a general direction to follow. Prior to 1701 Montreal and Three-Rivers were favorite French targets of the Iroquois.[49] Since the Sulpicians were based in Montreal, one might try to identify and gather biographical data about people captured in the Montreal area by the Oneidas. Limiting the search in this way leads almost immediately to the 1660s. Before then most attacks on Montreal were by the Mohawks; the Oneidas were rarely mentioned as attackers until 1650, and other than their names and place of capture, little data exist on people taken before 1660.[50]

Largely because of a paucity of data, only two people fit most of these criteria. The first is Charles Le Moyne de Longueuil.[51] Le Moyne, as he is usually referred to in the documents, settled on Montreal Island in 1646 and spent the rest of his life there. He was a trader, soldier, and interpreter for the government, was familiar with the Iroquois, was adopted into one of their clans, was captured by them in 1665, and was well regarded by the Sulpicians.[52] The description of his capture in one source even hints that Le Moyne may have been captured by the Oneidas. In his *Histoire de la colonie française* Abbé Étienne-Michel Faillon recorded Le Moyne's capture and the death of another Frenchman at the hands of the Iroquois and concluded his summary of events by stating, "finally, those of Oneida captured another one during the fall" who they later killed.[53] Unfortunately it is not clear if Abbé Faillon meant that the Oneidas captured "another" Frenchman (that is, captured a second person), or if he meant that they at last had joined the list of Iroquois tribes raiding into Montreal.

It is unlikely, however, that Le Moyne was the author of "Nation Iroquoise." Aside from the uncertainty of which group captured Le Moyne, he did not spend the winter among the Iroquois. Le Moyne was captured in either July or August of 1665 and was returned to the French by or before December of that year.[54] It appears that this was the only time he was an Iroquois captive. Nor does he seem to have reached a point where the Iroquois could trust him enough to let him travel unguarded with a pregnant woman. He was a belligerent captive and threatened the Iroquois with the wrath of a French army if he was not returned.[55]

The other person who appears to fit the author profile of "Nation Iroquoise" is René Cuillerier. In 1659, when he was about twenty years old, Cuillerier came to New France as an *engagé* to work at the Hôtel-Dieu at Montreal. In 1663 the Sulpicians were made *seigneurs* of the island, and in 1665 they gave Cuillerier a forty-five-acre grant of land.[56] That same year he married Marie Lucault, with whom he produced sixteen children. In 1675 he helped found the parish of Lachine, and by 1681 he had brought thirty-two acres of his original grant under cultivation. In 1689 he escaped the Iroquois attack that devastated the Lachine community and died at his home around 1712.[57]

Given his first experiences at Montreal, Cuillerier's willingness to stay on the island is to be admired. On 25 October 1661 he, along with a small number of troops and workers led by the soldier Claude de Brigeac and the Sulpician priest Guillaume Vignal, was attacked by the Oneidas.[58] Father Vignal was killed during the attack, and Cuillerier and Brigeac were taken to the Oneida village. Brigeac was later tortured to death among the Oneidas. Cuillerier was spared death, although not minor tortures, when a woman decided to adopt him to replace the brother Brigeac had killed in the recent raid. After some nineteen months among the Oneidas, Cuillerier took the opportunity of a hunting trip with the Mohawks to make his escape. Along with two other Frenchmen who were being held captive by the Mohawks, he made his way to New Netherland and from there back to New France.

Cuillerier's experience matches that of the author of "Nation Iroquoise" in every sense. His work at Montreal obviously put him in close contact with the priests of Saint-Sulpice who had picked the island as their base for missionary work. At the time of his capture Cuillerier was working for the Sulpicans gathering material for the construction of their new seminary. After the attack Cuillerier was mildly treated, compared to Brigeac, and was even released from his bonds to allow him to pray. The Oneidas obviously did not see him as much of a threat. Brigeac, even with a broken arm, was kept tied up. Cuillerier's treatment fits well with the "Nation Iroquoise" author's description of his being allowed to travel unguarded with a woman. Cuillerier was adopted by the Oneidas and obviously spent a significant amount of time among them. His role as assistant to the women of the clan may also account for his descriptions of their responsibilities. It could have been on his trip to the Mohawks and in his escape to New Netherland that he determined the distances from the Oneida villages to those of the Mohawks and from there to Orange, which inform the first part of "Nation Iroquoise," or he could have simply learned of the distances over time since he was among the Oneidas nineteen months.

A description of Cuillerier's captivity adventure, published by the Jesuits in their *Relation* of 1664–65, adds more evidence in support of Cuillerier as the author of "Nation Iroquoise."[59] Father Le Mercier, the "editor" of the *Relation* for that year, informed his readers that he was passing along the account in question several years after the fact because he had recently learned of it. He must have meant that he had only recently learned of the written account because the actual raid was reported in the *Relation* for 1661. The account published in 1664–65 describes Cuillerier's adventure in the third person but could only have been written by Cuillerier or, more likely, have been based upon Cuillerier's testimony.[60] Since Brigeac's death is recounted in this narrative and is told from the perspective of a person who witnessed it, and since Cuillerier was the only other Frenchman among the Oneidas at the time, it could only have been he who told the story. In this short captivity narrative the reader learns that Cuillerier saw one Frenchman tortured to death. An Algonquin captive, being tormented in much the same way as Brigeac, was also likely tortured to death. The "Nation Iroquoise" author saw eight men tortured to avenge one Oneida death. It may have been the need to avenge a death that had led to the attack in which Cuillerier was captured, or it may have been the death Brigeac caused that led to more hostilities. In any case, from 1661 to 1663 (the time of Cuillerier's captivity) various sources report at least eight French and twelve Natives killed by the Iroquois and at least eight Natives and an unspecified number of French taken captive.[61] An undetermined number of other raids are known to have taken place, but the results in terms of captives and killed are unknown. While one cannot be certain how many captives wound up among the Oneidas, it seems reasonable to suggest that Cuillerier would have had the opportunity to witness six more deaths by torture in his nineteen months with the Oneidas in addition to those he saw and described during the first few days of his captivity.

One other incident from the captivity narrative deserves mention. At one point during his captivity Cuillerier was threatened with death when an Iroquois pointed a pistol at his head and asked him whether he favored, presumably as a pastor, Father Le Moyne or Father Chaumonot.[62] Although there is no comparable incident in "Nation Iroquoise," the author of that document discussed the evil effects of alcohol on Iroquois society and related how, on several occasions, his life was threatened by intoxicated Iroquois.[63] The description of the life-threatening incident in Cuillerier's captivity narrative makes no mention of alcohol, but it does not seem too much to credit that intoxication had a role to play in the event. After all, one can hardly accept that a devout and sober Iroquois would express his loyalty to his faith and his particular French Jesuit priest by killing a Frenchman and fellow Catholic.

In the end though, one must concede that the evidence for Cuillerier as author of "Nation Iroquoise," while compelling, is circumstantial. Cuillerier emerges as author based upon a series of apparently reasonable deductions and assumptions derived from a measured reading of the evidence and by a process of eliminating other likely candidates from a list that is further circumscribed by lack of data. Could someone else have written or dictated "Nation Iroquoise"? The answer is, of course, yes: it is entirely possible.[64] Yet, it seems unlikely that "Nation Iroquoise" was written by someone other than René Cuillerier because, however much one must acknowledge the range of possibilities, one must concede that not all are knowable and that Cuillerier fits the available evidence too closely for it to be mere coincidence.

Even if one is prepared to concede that René Cuillerier is the author of "Nation Iroquoise," what evidence is there that the document was written at the time of his escape?[65] After all, he lived until about 1712. Conclusive evidence of the time of writing does not exist, but there is evidence (beyond the clearly seventeenth-century spelling in the document) to suggest "Nation Iroquoise" was written around 1664 or 1665 at the latest. Cuillerier's captivity narrative, published in the Jesuit's *Relation* of 1664–65, was obviously written sometime after he returned to the colony. Cuillerier was captured 25 October 1661 and lived among the Oneidas for nineteen months.[66] This means that he escaped around May 1663. Cuillerier then traveled to Fort Orange, Manhattan, and from there to Boston, to Quebec, and finally back to Montreal.[67] Thus, the earliest he could have been back in Montreal is late summer of 1663.[68] He might even have made it back in the early winter of 1664. The Jesuits published the captivity narrative in 1664–65, which indicates that they learned of the written account only in the late fall or early winter of 1664—after the *Rela-*

tion of 1663–64 had been completed and sent off to Paris with the fall 1664 fleet of ships carrying correspondence, documents, and furs back to France. The annual *Relations* reported events from the late fall and winter of one year to the late summer of the next in order for the reports to get back to France on the fall fleets. To be included in the *Relation* of 1663–64, the account would have had to be received by the Jesuit superior at Quebec by August 1664 at the latest. This would have allowed him time to write and edit it for publication and have it ready to sail with the fall 1664 fleet.[69] Either the Sulpicians did not ask Cuillerier to recount his story immediately, or they passed on the account to the Jesuits months after they had it. In any case, it is clear that by late 1664 the captivity account had been written up, most certainly by the Sulpicians.

Since "Nation Iroquoise" was written at the request of someone, and since sometime before the end of 1664 the Sulpicians had requested their *engagé* to recall his capture and what happened on his trip to Iroquoia for them to record, it seems reasonable to accept that the Sulpicians would also ask Cuillerier to tell them as much as he knew of the Iroquois who captured him since the Sulpicians had little firsthand contact with the Iroquois and were planning on opening missions to them. It is unlikely that Cuillerier could write. He was probably asked to respond to a series of questions, and his answers were written down by either a scribe or a priest. That process would help account for the lack of punctuation. If the scribe or priest was taking down information as he heard it, he probably did not pause to interrupt the speaker to ask when it was suitable to add periods and commas. A verbal report might also help explain some of the material that is out of place in the document, such as a description of women's hardiness in the section on mourning practices (although even written reports can appear to be disorganized since there is little accounting for personal sense of order and priorities).

The material covered in "Nation Iroquoise," while fitting the general pattern of ethnological topics written about in the 1600s, precisely addressed the needs of those planning new missions to the Iroquois.[70] The emphasis in "Nation Iroquoise" on describing councils—their variety and how they work—is particularly revealing. The Sulpicians must have learned, either on their own or based on the Jesuit experience, of the need to work within the Iroquois council structure if they hoped to persuade the Iroquois to grant them permission to proselytize among them.[71] The first Sulpician mission to the Iroquois was Kenté, near present-day Kingston, Ontario, and was begun in 1668. As well, the mid-to-late 1660s is the time of most intense Sulpician exploration and contact with Natives, and they clearly put an emphasis on recording their work. It is from this period that we have the first Sulpician histories in North America.[72] Given Sulpician plans, one would not expect that Cuillerier's adventure, and the wealth of information he possessed, would go unrecorded.

Be all that as it may, what does "Nation Iroquoise" tell us, and why is it important? In some instances the information provided about the Oneidas echoes what other known sources have to say about Iroquois society, although if the dating of "Nation Iroquoise" holds up, one can contend that later sources confirm what Cuillerier first observed.[73] For example, he began his account by describing the locations of Iroquois villages and the relative distances from one to another. The topography, fertility of soil, as well as the fauna and the vegetation and crops found in Iroquoia, all came in for favorable comment. As is usual, Cuillerier compared all that he saw both with France and New France. The material here is in line with that in other seventeenth-century French accounts. So too are some of the observations on religion, mourning practices, roles of women, and the generally flattering assessments of Iroquois character.[74] In this sense "Nation Iroquoise" is important precisely because it confirms what is known from other sources about other Iroquois tribes and shows that the cultural patterns of the Oneidas were similar.

The real importance of "Nation Iroquoise," however, rests in the details that add to our understanding of particular aspects of Iroquois society. Often Cuillerier's observations provide evidence of long-suspected Iroquois practices. Take, for example, Cuillerier's commentary on Iroquois governance and the relationship between governance and the clan system. Like Lafitau after him, Cuillerier noted the connection between the two, but unlike Lafitau he was not concerned with rooting his observations in classical literature or with making larger points about Iroquoian cultural links to the ancient past. Thus Cuillerier's analysis of governance reads like a "how to" primer, with an emphasis on the process. More significantly, Cuillerier makes it clear that should a matter decided in council be of significance to other tribes, two members of each clan were selected to go to other villages because it was through clan affiliations that contacts with other villages were made. Many students of the Iroquois have probably come to the conclusion that it was for this reason that representatives of each clan were selected on such occasions, but Cuillerier's analysis provides clear evidence for this belief.

Cuillerier also furnishes evidence that relates to the debate about the longevity of the Iroquois Confederacy. Over the last few years some Iroquoianists have argued that although the famous League of the Iroquois may be quite ancient, the Confederacy of the Iroquois was a relatively recent development.[75] The question of whether the League of the Iroquois and the Confederacy are one and the same, and the relative age of each, if they are different, is unlikely to be resolved soon. Yet, Cuillerier's work does allow one to contend that the League/Confederacy dates to at least 1660. Writing in 1724, Lafitau, for example, described practices that have been taken as evidence of the existence of the League/Confederacy and of honorary titles.[76] Cuillerier, based on his experiences some sixty years before Lafitau, also spoke of the existence of honorary titles, raising up of chiefs whose names were announced to the other tribes of the Iroquois, and concluded with the observation that "distinguished men die in that country as in ours, but their names reign on." In some form, what Lafitau described in the early eighteenth century also existed in the mid-seventeenth century.[77]

In short, then, it seems safe to conclude that it was René Cuillerier who was captured and adopted into the Oneida nation, and who left us a record of what he learned and experienced after he was made "but one people" with the Oneidas. His legacy is one of the earliest and most well rounded "ethnographic" analyses of Iroquois culture. It predates Joseph-François Lafitau's *Moeurs des Sauvages ameriquains* by as much as sixty years and was written before the Jesuits established enduring missions in Iroquoia in the late 1660s. It is also a far more complete attempt at cultural analysis than that left by Pierre Radisson and Pierre Boucher, who also wrote about the Iroquois around 1660.[78]

Part 2. The Document

Notes on Transcription and Translation

Note about the Transcription

"Nation Iroquoise" was transcribed from a microfilm copy of the document held in the Bibliothèque Mazarine, manuscrit 1964. In 1931 Canada's national archives ordered a handwritten transcript copy (National Archives of Canada, Manuscript Group 7, IV, vol. 1964). The present transcription has been checked against both the original and against the 1931 transcript. Some minor errors were found in the 1931 transcript. All of the changes consist of missing or additional letters and accents. At times the transcriber appears to have forgotten herself and used the twentieth-century spelling of some words.

The present transcription is a "diplomatic" one and faithfully follows the original in the Biblothèque Mazarine—warts and all. Missing words and punctuation have not been added, nor have spelling, grammar, capitalization, and accent placement been corrected. Nonetheless, a few minor adjustments had to be made. It has not appeared important to replicate the symbol that looks like a number eight written sideways with a looping line through it, which the copyist placed after each section title. Also, in the original document paragraph breaks, while few, are readily evident because of where words end on the last line and not because the first sentence of the new paragraph is indented. In copying the text it was impossible to end the printed version of a sentence as conveniently. For that reason the first line of each new paragraph has been indented.

The numbers in brackets in the transcription refer to the folio pages in the original document. The verso pages were not numbered in the original.

Note about the Translation

The goal of the following translation has been to remain faithful to the style, syntax, wording, and intent of the original French document and still make it intelligible to modern readers. This aim is made difficult because it is unlikely that the author of "Nation Iroquoise" had much of a formal education, and one cannot expect to find, and does not find, a sophisticated vocabulary and polished grammatical skills in the document. Thus, in places ideas are conflated, and meaning is sometimes ambiguous. All of this is either complicated by, or the result of, the lack of clearly punctuated sentences.[1] This general maxim of translating is particularly true for documents such as "Nation Iroquoise" where the observer describes cultural practices, values, and customs, and when not all modern authorities agree about what those practices might mean.

For all of these reasons, the text is translated as literally as possible so that it reflects the original style, wording, and, hopefully, intent of the French *mémoire*.[2] Punctuation, however, has been introduced to create clear sentences. In order to make sense of the unpunctuated French text one has to make decisions about what constitutes a complete thought or a sentence, and thus one introduces "mental punctuation" to complete the translation. Because such decisions were made in the translation, it seemed disingenuous not to make that clear in the English text. In some places a period can be placed after any one of several words, and the preceding and subsequent "sentences" will still make sense. Thus, adding punctuation introduces a significant level of editorial interference with the text and increases the opportunities to alter the original author's intent. I take some comfort in the fact that the University of Nebraska Press has allowed me to provide the French text alongside the translation, so readers will be able to consult the original text.

Other changes and additions could not be avoided. For the reasons discussed in the note on transcription, the first lines of new paragraphs have been indented. If clarity absolutely demanded an extra word, it has been silently added except in the case of a description of a cultural practice, where additions have been indicated in a note. Gallicisms, expressions that make sense in French but not in English, can often be made intelligible without distorting the author's meaning or "voice." Little is gained by a literal translation in such instances. Still, the preferred approach has been to err on the side of caution. For example, *donne sa voix,* which translates as "gives his voice," can be rendered as "gives his view" or "expresses his opinion" or "voices his opinion." The French makes sense as written, but the literal translation may appear awkward to modern readers. Yet, even in the French of the period it could have been better expressed. Raudot, for example, rendered this as *donne son avis,* which translates as "gives his opinion."[3] Is the occasional awkward syntax in "Nation Iroquoise" a function of the author's linguistic skills, or is it because he is attempting to provide, in French, a uniquely Iroquois expression or phrase? In a number of places the author indicates that he is rendering in French a specific Iroquois term. How many other times may he have done the same thing inadvertently or simply overlooked mentioning it? Rather than risk the loss of this potential insight into Iroquois culture, a fairly literal translation was chosen in such instances.

Nation Iroquoise

The Iroquois Nation

[f. 1r]

Abregé des vies et moeurs et autres Particularitez de La Nation Irokoise laquelle est diviseé en Cinq villages. Sçavoir Agnez, Onney8t, Nontagué, Goyog8an et Sonnont8an

Le Premier village qui est aniers est voisin d'orange, le 2eme qui est onneyoutte est a 25 lieües de distance en montant au Sud-oüest, le 3eme qui est nontagué est a 18 lieües d'oñeyoutte le 4eme qui est goyogoüan est a 20 lieuës de nontagué et les Sonnontoüans qui sont

<1r>

Abridgement of the Lives and Customs and Other Particulars of the Iroquois Nation which is divided into Five Villages, namely, Agnez, Oney8t, Nontagué, Goyog8an, and Sonnont8an

The first village, which is Aniers, neighbors on Orange.[1] The second, which is Onneyoutte, is 25 leagues away moving uphill to the southwest.[2] The third, which is Nontagué, is 18 leagues from Onneyoutte. The fourth, which is Goyogoüan, is 20 leagues from Nontagué, and the Sonnontoüans, who constitute

[f. 1v]
les derniers villages sont éloignés de goyogoüan de 12 lieuës de sorte quils occupent en longueur plus de 75 lieuës de païs je veux dire depuis le premier vilage[1] jusqu'au dernier. Ces terres dont ils sont les maîtres s'estendent autant qu'ils veulent. Il faut remarquer que quoique ce païs la soit remply de montagnes il est vray de dire que les terres y sont merueilleuses leur blé d'inde y vient tres beau ainsy que tout ce qu'ils y sément les arbres y sont d'une prodigieuse grosseur marque éuidente de la bonté de la terre le chataigner y est plus gros que celuy d'europe le fruit en est plus petit que le nôtre il s'y trouue des paîches sauuages des meuriers de deux sortes rouge et blanc les noix y sont en abondance de plusieurs sortes et il s'en trouue d'aussi boñes qu'en france mais il n'y en a pas beaucoup attendu que les sauuages coup̄ent les arbres pour en auoir le fruit ils en usent de la sorte à l'egard des chataigners et meuriers

<IV>

the last villages, are removed from Goyogoüan by 12 leagues, in such a way that they occupy over 75 leagues of the country's latitude; I mean from the first to the last village.[3] The lands of which they are the masters stretch out as far as they want. It must also be observed that although that country is full of mountains, it is true to say that the lands there are marvellous;[4] their corn comes in very fine along with everything that they plant there. The trees there are of a prodigious size, an obvious sign of the goodness of the soil. The chestnut tree there is larger than that of Europe, but the fruit of it is smaller than ours. One finds wild peaches there and mulberries of two types: red and white. The nuts there are plentiful, of several varieties, and some are found to be as good as in France, but there are not many, given that the natives[5] cut the trees to have the fruit of them. They practice this usage with respect to the chestnut and the mulberry.

[f. 2r]
la vigne sauuage y est abondante le raisin en est tres beau et bien fourny de plusieurs Especes[2] qui meurit parfaitement bien s'il étoit affranchy je le croirois aussy bon que le nôtre il y a aussi des prunes de qualité differente j'en ay veu de blanches coṁe les nôtres que nous noṁons darille qui sont tres boñes il s'y trouue beaucoup de poṁiers qui se chargent plus de fruit que ceux que nous cultiuons mais il n'est pas bon les freizes, framboizes, et deux especes de meures des ronces y sont en abondance aussi bien que d'autres fruits qui sont incoñus en europe il s y trouue des àuelines et noisettes en quantité.

Ces terres sont entre coupees de petites riuieres dont la plus grande partie porte canots et batteaux il s'y trouue aussy quantité de lacs dont ils retirent de grandes douceurs par le prodigieux nombre de poissons qu'ils y preñent coṁe Saumons truites brochets poissons dorés

<2r>

The wild vine is abundant there. The grape of it is very fine and well furnished with several species that ripen perfectly well. If it were transplanted,[6] I would believe it as good as ours. There are also plums of varying quality. I have seen white ones, like ours that we call *darille*,[7] which are very good. Many apple trees are found there that are more laden with fruit than the ones which we cultivate, but it is not good. Strawberries, raspberries, and two types of blackberries are there in abundance, as well as other fruits that are unknown in Europe. One finds filberts and hazel nuts there in great quantity.

These lands are intersected with small rivers, of which the majority carry canoes and boats. One finds there also a large number of lakes from which they draw great comfort through the prodigious number of fish that they take there, such as salmon, trout, pike, walleye pike,

[f. 2v]
achigans anguilles et tous autres qui les nourissent plus de 4 mois de l'anneé.

Les animaux de plusieurs especes y sont en nombre sauoir Cerfs Cheureüils Ours Originaux Castors Loutres Loups Loups-seruiérs Renards Martes Pécants Vizons Bellereaux Porc-espics Rats musqués Rats de bois Ecureüils volans Ecureüils roux Ecureüils noirs et gris qui sont beaucoup plus gros que les autres dont ces sauuages se font des robbes de la peau fort estimeé entre eux les liéures y sont plus petits que les nôtres.

Les Dindes Sauuages Perdrix Griues Etournaux et toutes d'oiseaux[3] se trouuent en quantité dans l'étendüe de ce païs les tourtes y sont d'un grand secours par la quantité prodigieuse qu'ils en preñent auec des filets dont ils se nourissent plus de 2 mois de l'añée. Il y a quantité d'oizeaux de riuiere de toutes les espéces de

<2V>

bass, eels, and all others which nourish them for more than four months of the year.

Animals of many species are numerous there, namely elk, deer, bear, moose, beavers, otters, wolves, lynxes, foxes, martens, fishers, minks, badgers, porcupines, muskrats, "rats of the woods,"[8] flying squirrels, red squirrels, and black and gray squirrels that are much larger than the others, from whose pelts, much esteemed among them, these natives make themselves robes. The hares there are smaller than ours.

The wild turkeys, partridges, thrushes, starlings,[9] and all kinds[10] of birds are found in great quantity throughout the length of this land. The wild pigeons there are a great help on account of the prodigious quantity of them that they capture with nets, and by which they nourish themselves for more than two months of the year. There is an abundance of river birds in Canada of all the species of

[f. 3r]
celles que nous auons dans le Canada et j'ose auancer qu'ils sont en plus grand nombre attendu qu'ils ne sont pas si chassés que parmy nous.

Voila monsieur à peu pres ce que je puis vous marquer pour vous doñer une idée des terres que possede cette nation[4]

Voyons maintenant leur Religion

La religion de ces peuples consiste en bien peu de chose ils ne recoñoissent point d'autre Dieu que le Soleil et c'est a luy a qui ils s'adressent dans toutes leurs nécessités tant pour la guerre que pour la chasse c'est pourquoy ils n'entrepreñent jamais rien sans auoir doñe auparauant à fumer a cet astre le priant de dissiper les nüages qui l'enuiroñent qui est vn presage assuré pour eux qu'ils croyent être regardés de bon oeil de cette diuinité lors qu'il leur accorde. Ils ne sauoient ce que c'estoit que priere deuant que les Reuerends peres

<3r>

those that we have, and I dare suggest that they are in greater number, considering that they are not as hunted as they are among us.

There, sir, is approximately what I can record for you in order to give you an idea of the lands which this nation possesses.

Now Let Us Take a Look at Their Religion

The religion of these peoples consists of very few things. They do not recognize any other God than the Sun, and it is to it that they address themselves in all their needs, as much for war as for the hunt. That is why they never undertake anything without first having offered smoke to this heavenly body, beseeching it to disperse the clouds that surround it. This is a certain omen for them, by which they believe themselves to be regarded with a favorable eye by this divinity when it is granted to them.[11] They did not know what prayer was before the Reverend Jesuit

[f. 3v]
Jesuites y eussent estes lesquels n'ont rien negligé pour leur faire embrasser. Mais comẽ leurs vices capitaux sont tout a fait op̃osés a nôtre religion cela na pas laissé de diminuër le fruit que deuoient esperer de si zellés missioñaires L'yurognerie a toujours esté vn grand obstacle pour ceux qui y ont presché l'euangile.

Les filles et feẽs y sont trés debauchées et ne courent aucun risque que d'estre abandoñées de leurs maris ce qui arriue souuent et les filles addoñeés a cette passion ne se marient queres d'ordinaire ces Sauuages aiment la vertu sans la vouloir pratiquer Il n'est point de regle sans exception ainsy il s'y trouue des ménages qu'il n'y a que la mort seule qui puisse les separer. Ceux ou celles qui sont atteints de vol dans ces païs la ne sont pas plus estimés que parmy nous et ces Sauuages en font quelque fois justice La Medisance y regne beaucoup et cepen-

<3v>

Fathers had been there; the latter neglected nothing to make them embrace it. But as their capital vices are completely opposed to our religion, that has not failed to diminish the fruit which ought to be hoped for from such zealous missionaries. Drunkenness has always been a great obstacle for those who have preached the gospel there.

The girls and women there are very wanton and do not run any risk except of being abandoned by their husbands, which often happens. And, ordinarily, the girls given to this passion hardly ever marry. These natives love virtue without wishing to practice it. There is no rule without any exception; thus one finds there couples whom only death alone can separate. Those men or women who are convicted[12] of theft in those regions are no more esteemed than among us, and these natives sometimes treat them as they deserve. Slander is very prevalent there and yet

[f. 4r]

dant n'a point de suittes que dans l'yurognerie. La Jalousie y trouue sa place aussi bien que l'enuie, point de bataille parmy eux à moins que l'eau de vie ne s'en mesle tenant pour indigne celuy qui se fâcheroit sans être yure cependant il est vray de dire que quelques fois le mary et la feme se battent, et qui cause cela? quelque fois la jalousie dans d'autre temps l'yuresse sans que le plus souuent cela porte a consequence. Quoi qu'ils n'aiment pas beaucoups les menteurs je crois qu'il n'y a point de païs ou on ment mieux que dans ces lieux la. Les vieillards femes et filles parlent de la bagatelle capable de faire rougir les jeunes gens les plus debordés les jeunes homes sont assés reserués sur ce sujet.

De La maniere Dont ils Tienent Leurs Conseils

Il Faut remarquer qu'ils en ont de plu-

<4r>

bears no consequences except in drunkenness. Jealousy finds its place there as well as envy, but there is no fighting among them unless brandy is mixed up with it. The one who would lose his temper without being drunk is held to be shameful. Yet, it is true to say that sometimes the husband and the wife fight, and what causes that? Sometimes jealousy, at other times drunkenness, for the most part, without that bearing any consequences. Although they do not like liars very much, I believe that there is no country where they lie better than in those places. The elderly, women, and girls talk about sex in a manner capable of making the most dissipated young people blush. The young men are sufficiently reserved on this subject.

Of the Manner in Which They Hold Their Councils

It must be observed that they have several

[f. 4v]
sieurs Sortes attendu que chaque village est composé de plusieurs familles les vns plus et les autres moins. Celuy donc ou celle qui a quelques propositions a faire com̄ence par assembler les anciens de sa famille et si c'est quelque chose qui regarde les guerriers on fait venir un ou deux capitaines de cette même famille pour être témoins de la chose qu'on propose chacun y doñe sa voix d'une maniere tres Serieuse aprés quoy ils conuieñent des faits cela étant finy vn ancien député par eux va inuiter les autres familles je veux dire anciens et chefs de guerre sup̄osé que la chose le demande ainsy toutes ces formalités se font d'une maniere tres hoñête ce qui ma Surpris plusieurs fois de voir en cela leur Conduite. enfin étant assemblés cette proposition paroît sur le tapis aux inuités par Colliers quand la chose est de consequence aprés quoy ceux qui ont proposé se retirent

<4v>

types of them, considering that each village is composed of many families,[13] some more and others less. He then, or she, who has some propositions to make begins by assembling the elders of his or her family, and if it is something that concerns the warriors, one or two captains of this same family are summoned to be witnesses to the thing being proposed. Each one there gives his opinion in a very serious manner, after which they agree upon the procedure.[14] That being finished, an elder appointed by them goes to invite the other families, I mean the elders and war chiefs, supposing that the thing requires it. In this way, all these formalities are done in a very seemly manner; it has surprised me many times to see their conduct in that. At last, being assembled, this proposition appears on the mat[15] to those invited by strings of wampum[16]—when the matter is significant. Whereupon, those who have made the proposal withdraw

[f. 5r]
et s'en vont a l'écart a vne distance capable de les empêcher d'entendre ce que diront ceux qu'ils ont attirés pour l'examen de leurs propositions il arriue quelques fois qu'ils ne décident point sur l'heure même et d'ordinaire leur décision ne se fait promptement que dans une affaire presseé. Si dans la décison on juge à propos d'en doñer auis aux autres villages cela se fait avec ceremonie comme par exemple Oñey8t qui est composé de trois familles sauoir la famille du loup la famille de la tortüe et celle de l'ours dans ce cas ils députent vn ou deux des principaux de chaque famille pour aller com̃uniquer à leurs alliés leurs projects.

Conseils Pour ce qui concerne La Guerre

Il faut remarquer que la nation Irokoise est celle de tous les Sauuages la plus belliqueuse & si le françois ne s'etoit point éta-

<5r>

and go off at a distance sufficient to hinder them from understanding what those whom they have drawn to the examination of their propositions will say. It happens sometimes that they do not reach a decision at that very moment, and ordinarily they do not make a prompt decision except in an urgent matter. If in the decision they judge it appropriate to give notice of it to the other villages,[17] that is done with ceremony, as for example among the Oney8t, which is composed of three families,[18] namely the family of the Wolf, the family of the Turtle, and that of the Bear. In this case, they appoint one or two of the principal men of each family to go and explain their plans to their allies.

Councils of War

It must be observed that the Iroquois Nation is the most warlike of all the native peoples, and if the Frenchman had not been established

[f. 5v]
bly dans ce Païs il ne faut pas douter qu'ils ne se fussent rendus les maîtres de toutes les autres nations sa perte a comencée lorsque l'enuie leur a pris de nous faire la guerre c'est surquoy ces Sauuages raisonent quelques fois sans pourtant y vouloir réfleschir.

Les Conseils pour la guerre se font d'ordinaire le plus secrettement qu'il est possible cela se fait par vne assembleé des anciens de chaque village il s'y joint dans ce Conseil des femes qui ont leur voix et qui décident come les vieillards ils mettent sur la natte pour me servir de leur terme tous les griefs qu'ils croyent auoir contre la nation qu'ils veulent fraper et aprés quils ont decidés sur ce sujet il se fait une autre assembleé ou les chefs de guerre sont apellés alors vn orateur choisy de l'assembleé harangue les Chefs de guere et leur fait conoître la necessité indispensable qu'ils ont de se venger contre ceux dont ils croyent auoir été insultés;

<5v>

in this country, they would have made themselves, undoubtedly, the masters of all the other nations. Their ruin began when the fancy for making war on us took hold of them. That is what these natives argue about sometimes without, for all that, wanting to reflect upon it.

The Councils of War are ordinarily arranged as secretly as possible. That is done by an assembly of the elders from each village. Some women who have their own voice in these matters, and who make decisions like the old men, join them in this Council. They place upon the mat (to avail myself of their expression) all the grievances that they believe they have against the nation that they wish to strike. And after they have decided on this matter, another assembly is held, to which the war chiefs are summoned. Then a speaker, chosen from the assembly, harangues the war chiefs and informs them of the absolute necessity of avenging themselves upon those by whom they believe themselves to have been offended.

[f. 6r]
La harangue finie les principaux chefs de guerre s'assemblent a vne distance du rond des anciens et font leurs reflexions sur la harangue qui leur a esté faite et aprés auoir décidé de la résponse qu'ils doiuent faire ils retournent a leur premiere place dont l'un d'entr'eux qui doit parler se leue et repete tout ce qui a été dit cy deuant aprés quoy il leur déclare ce qu'ils ont conclû cela finy il chante Sa chanson de guerre et chacun y chante la sieñe Captitaines, Soldats, et les anciens aussy. Voila coṁe s'allume leur guerre & le plus souuent ils la font a ceux qui ne leur ont jamais fait aucun mal. toutes ces ceremonies faites ils conuiennent du jour qu'ils doiuent partir et pour lors chacun s'en retourne a son village et y estans arriués ils font assembler tous les guerriers dans une Cabane d'un chef de guerre qui est d'ordinaire pour ces sortes d'assembleés. enfin quand ils y sont tous rendus vn de ces anciens leur

<6r>

When the speech is finished, the principal war chiefs gather together at a distance from the elders' circle and reflect upon the speech which was made to them. And after having decided upon the response which they should make, they return to their former place, from which the one from among them who is to speak[19] gets up and repeats everything which was said up to that point, after which he declares to them what they have concluded. That finished, he chants his war song, and each one there chants his own: captains, soldiers, and the elders too. Behold how their war is kindled, and most often they wage it upon those who have never done them any harm. With the completion of all these ceremonies, they agree upon the day when they ought to depart, and until that time, each one returns to his village. And having arrived home, they summon all the warriors into a war chief's lodge, which is normal for these kinds of gatherings. Finally, when they have all gotten themselves there, one of these elders tells

[f. 6v]

raconte ce qui a esté projetté ayant finy il entoñe sa chanson de guerre les Spectateurs en font autant chacun a leur tour il faut sauoir que la Chaudiere de guerre boüille pendant qu'ils chantent elle se noñe chaudiere de guerre attendu que c'est pour ce dessein qu'elle a esté mise au feu le festin finy vn vieillard va faire le cry dans le village par lequel il exhorte les feñes et filles de trauailler incessañent aux prouisions nécessaires pour cette expediton elles le font auek vne promptitude surprenante ce que j'ay admiré plusieurs fois de voir (non à cela seul) leur obeïssance enfin le jour assigné pour le départ arriué ces femes et filles se chargent de prouisions de ces guerriers et leurs portent a dix ou quinze lieües de leurs villages ou ils s'arrêtent quelque fois pour chasser ou ils tuënt cheureüils cerfs Ours et Dindes que ces feñes ap-

<6v>

them what has been planned. Having finished, he intones his war song. The spectators do likewise, each in their turn. It is necessary to know that the war kettle boils while they sing. It is called the war kettle considering that it is for this purpose that it was placed on the fire.[20] The feast over, an old man goes to raise the cry[21] in the village, by which he exhorts the women and girls to work ceaselessly at the provisions needed for this expedition. They do this with a surprising promptitude, which I have many times admired (and not only that), seeing their dutifulness. Finally, the day assigned for the departure arrives and these women and girls load themselves up with the provisions of these warriors and carry them[22] up to ten or fifteen leagues from their villages where they sometimes stop to hunt and[23] kill deer, elk, bears, and turkeys, which these women

[f. 7r]

portent a leurs Villages les Capitaines et Soldats continüent leur route dont la campagne est quelque fois de 4 a 5 et 6 mois attendu qu'ils ne font que de tres petites journées et ne marchent jamais d'un temps sombre a moins que ce ne soit dans vne affaire pressée et souuent tous leurs beaux projets se terminent quelques fois a 4 ou 5 cheueleures & autant de prisoñiers a trois ou quatre cents hom̃es qu'ils sont de ce party ils s'en reuieñent aussi glorieux que s'ils auoient gagné une bataille entiere.

Pour leur rendre toute la justice qui leur ap̄artient il est vray qu'ils ont enleué des villages entiers ou il y auoit jusqu'a douze et quinze cents ames qu'ils on partagés par nation et ensuite adoptés dans leurs familles je veux dire les jeunes persoñes car fort rarement ils doñent la vie aux hom̃es faits appréhendant qu'ils ne puissent s'accoûtumer chez eux et qu'ils ne s'esquiuent

<7r>

carry to their villages. The captains and soldiers continue along their route, whose campaign is sometimes from four to five and six months long, considering that they only make very short treks and never walk in gloomy weather, unless it is an urgent affair. And often all their good plans sometimes end up with four or five scalps and as many prisoners for[24] the three or four hundred men that make up this party. They come back from it as glorious as if they had won an entire battle.

In order to render them all the justice which is their due, one should say that it is true that they have taken[25] whole villages where there were up to twelve and fifteen hundred souls whom they divided by nation[26] and then adopted into their families; I mean the young people, for very rarely do they let grown men live, fearing that the latter cannot grow accustomed to the life among them and that they may slip away.

[f. 7v]
le feu est la fin de la vie de ces pauures malheureux qui sont brûlés plus cruellement que tout ce que je pourrois vous en dire j'ay esté témoin de plusieurs a qui ce malheur est arriué et en outre de huit hom̃es tant françois que Sauuages qui ont finy leurs jours dans ces tourmens terribles et cela causé par la mort d'un seul homme de la nation d'oñey8t qui auoit esté tué en guerre;

Conseils Particuliers Pour La Guerre

Ces Sortes de Conseils se font tout autrement que les autres com̃e par exemple celuy ou celle qui aura perdu son fils son mary ou son neueu il leur est permis d'en tirer vengeance et voicy com̃e ils entrepreñent la chose par vn

<7v>

The fire[27] is the end of the life of these poor unfortunates who are burned more cruelly than I could possibly tell you about. I have been a witness to several to whom this misfortune has occurred and, in addition, to eight men, both French and native, who have ended their days in these terrible torments—and that caused by the death of a single man from the Oney8t nation who had been killed in battle.

Special Councils of War

These types of Councils are done very differently from the others, as, for example, in the case of a man or a woman who will have lost a son, a husband, or a nephew, he or she is allowed to take revenge[28] for it. And here is how they tackle the matter by means of a

[f. 8r]
Collier qu'ils doñent a vn guerrier qu'ils coñoissoient être amy du deffunt et Souuent c'est ceux qui sont d'une autre famille qui vengent cette mort ces sortes de colliers ne Se refusent jamais attendu que c'est faire hoñeur a celuy a qui on le presente celuy donc qui est choisy pour cela a la soin d'enrôller les Soldats qu'il luy faut pour cette expedition toutes sortes de mortes se peuuent venger de cette maniere chés eux car ils n'examinent point Si le deffunt est mort sur sa natte ou si il a esté tué en guerre cela leur est égal souuent ils inuitent des guerriers Des[5] autres villages pour se joindre a eux ce qui leur est accordé ils sortent du village en tirant chacun vn coups de fusil qui Signifie leur départ ils vont quelques fois 2 ou 300 lieuës pour venger ces sortes de morts ou bien Souuent ils ne reüssissent pas et quand ils ont faits

<8r>

string of wampum[29] which they give to a warrior whom they know to be a friend of the deceased. And often those who are from another family avenge this death. These kinds of strings are never refused, considering that it honors the one to whom they present it. The one, then, who is chosen for that task assumes the responsibility of recruiting the soldiers that he requires for this expedition. All kinds of deaths can be avenged among them in this way, for they do not examine whether the deceased died on his mat or if he was killed in war. It is all the same for them. Often they invite warriors from other villages to join with them, which is granted to them. They go out of the village, each one firing a gunshot, which signifies their departure. Sometimes, they go two or three hundred leagues to avenge these kinds of deaths, where they very often fail. And when they have taken

[f. 8v]
quelques prisoñiers ils en doñent vn pour r'emplacer le deffunt dont la vie dépend de celuy ou celle a qui il aura esté doñé

Mais pour ces sortes de morts peu sont exemts du feu. J'ay obmis a vous marquer quelque chose de la reception qu'ils font a ces pauures prisoñiers. Celuy donc qui co-m̃ande le party destache d'ordinaire deux couriers pour auertir le village du coup qu'ils ont fait ainsy que du jour qu'ils y doiuent arriuer et lorsque ces deux deputés ap̄ro-chent de leurs villages ils font de Distance en Distance au-tant de cris com̃e de cheueleures et prisoñiers qu'ils ont faits dans ce party je vous diray aussy qu'en ces sortes de partis on perd du monde. Ces Sortes de cris Se font tout au-trement ce qu'ils sauent tres bien discerner les anciens in-terrogent ces deux nouueaux arrivés sauoir si ceux qu'ils on laissés ont des viures

<8v>

some prisoners, they present one of them to replace the deceased, whose life depends upon the man or woman to whom he will have been given.

But for these kinds of deaths, few are exempt from the fire. I have omitted to note down for you something about the reception that they give to these poor prisoners. He, then, who commands the party ordinarily dispatches two runners to alert the village of the strike they have made, as well as of the day when they ought to arrive there. And when these two envoys approach their villages, at periodic intervals they make as many cries as there were scalps and prisoners taken by them in this sally. I will also tell you that one loses a lot of people in these types of sallies. These kinds of cries are done quite differently, which they can discern very well. The elders interrogate these two new arrivals, in order to ascertain if those whom they have left behind have sufficient

[f. 9r]
suffisam̃ent pour les amener jusqu'au village et S'ils disent qu'ils en manquent aussitôt on détache du monde pour leur en porter enfin le jour vient qu'ils doiuent arriuer hom̃es fem̃es et enfans sortent du village et vont au deuant d'eux quelques fois plus d'une demie lieüe en faisant des cris capables de faire dresser le cheueux Ces pauures malheureux prisoñiers tombent entre leurs mains a qui ils doñent la salüade (c'est leur terme) et com̃ent les salüent-ils? par Coups de bâtons et de pierres de coups de Coûteaux et a coups de dents ils leurs arrachent les ongles ce n'est pas cette nation seule qui obserue cette mauuaise maxime de mal traiter ainsy les prisoñiers ce sont tous les Sauuages en general a la verité les vns bien plus cruels que les autres;

Conseils Pour aller Pleurer Les Morts.

<9r>

supplies to last them up to the village. And if they say that they lack them, immediately they dispatch some people to bring them some. At last the day comes when they ought to arrive. Men, women, and children depart from the village and go before them, sometimes by more than half a league, raising cries fit to make one's hair stand on end. These poor unfortunate prisoners fall into their hands, to whom they give the greeting (that is their term)[30]. And how do they greet them? By blows from sticks and stones. Striking with knives and teeth, they tear out their nails. It is not this nation alone which observes this faulty maxim of treating prisoners badly in this way; all the natives in general do it, in truth some being much more cruel than others.

Councils for Going to Mourn the Dead

[f. 9v]

Quand il arriue que quelque considerable d'un village est mort cela vient aussy tôt a la coñoissance des autres pour lors il se fait vne assembleé des autres villages qui tous d'un com̃un accord fournissent à ceux qui sont députés pour aller pleurer le deffunt de la porcelaine ou bien quelques hardes ou peltries en la place cela se fait auec vne grande ceremonie et d'une maniere tres serieuse et en faisant leur complimens ils couurent le corps du mort de ce qu'ils ont porté cette ceremonie étant finie de ceux dont je parle vn ancien du village du deffunt les remercie tres hoñêtement auec ap̄robation de la nation de la part qu'ils ont pris a la perte qu'ils ont fait leurs ciuilitez acheuées tant d'une part que d'autre chacun se retire chés soy et quelques temps aprés on trauaille a Substituer vn autre de la famille du deffunt pour reprendre son nom cela

<9v>

When it happens that someone of considerable importance in a village has died, it immediately comes to the attention of the others; in this case[31] an assembly is constituted from the other villages who, all by common agreement, furnish some wampum[32] or even some clothing or furs, in the place, to those who are appointed to go and mourn for the deceased. That is done with great ceremony and in a very serious manner. And while paying their respects, they cover the body of the dead man with what they have brought. When this ceremony of those of whom I am speaking has come to an end, an elder from the village of the deceased thanks them very sincerely, with the nation's approval, for the role that they have assumed in the loss they have experienced.[33] Their civilities completed, as much on one side as the other, each one withdraws to his home. And, sometime later, they work toward substituting another member of the family of the deceased in order to take up again his name. That

[f. 10r]
étant fait ils vont le com̃uniquer aux quatre autres villages dont il leur en Coûte quelques Colliers de porcelaine; les hom̃es distingués meurent dans ce païs la com̃e dans le nôtre mais leurs noms regnent toûjours.

De Leur Esprit

De Toutes les nations que nous auons en ce païs il n'y a que le huron qui les surpasse pour l'esprit j'ay toujours oüy dire par les RR PP. Jesuites que l'yrokois en auoit beaucoup et cela a paru en bien des endroits car ils ont toûjours sçu tromper les autres sans se laisser tromper eux mêmes ils ont la memoire tres bon̄e et s'ap̄liquent beaucoup a raconter leurs affaires passées c'est pourquoy ils n'oublient jamais rien point de nation au monde plus politique que celle la et qui sache mieux se gouuerner; ils Sont

<101>

being done, they go to communicate it to the other four villages,[34] which costs them some wampum strings. Distinguished men die in that country as in ours, but their names reign forever.

Concerning Their Intelligence

Of all the nations that we have in this country, only the Hurons surpass them in intelligence. I have always heard the Reverend Jesuit Fathers say that the Iroquois had a lot of it, and that has become apparent in many places,[35] for they have always known how to deceive others without allowing themselves to be deceived. They have very good memories and often take great pains to recount their past affairs. That is why they never forget anything. There is no more politic nation in the world than that one, and which would know better how to govern itself. They are

[f. 10v]
toûjours d'une tres grande intelligence les vns avec les autres quand il s'agit de porter des nouuelles d'un village a l'autre ils n'ont qu'a com̃ander et aussitôt ils sont obeïs il n'y a jamais de refus soit pour la découuerte ou pour la chasse et pour tout[6] autre chose ils sont tres actifs et fort preuoyans et adroits a tout ce qu'ils veulen faire raisoñant tres juste sur tout ce qui les Concernent[7] laborieux sur tout ce qui peut leur faire plaisir ils s'attachent beaucoup a faire quantité de blé dinde féues et autres choses qu'ils sément aussy c'est pourquoy ils n'ont point de peine à quitter leurs villages pour aller faire la guerre aux autres nations attendu qu'ils laissent a leurs familles tout ce qui est nécessaire pour leur Subsistance voila l'auantage qu'ils ont sur une partie des autres nations que tant s'en faut qu'ils soient Si laborieux que l'Irokois, ils

<10v>

always in extensive communication with one another. When it is a question of carrying some news from one village to another, they have only to make a command, and immediately they are obeyed. There is never any refusal, either to perform a discovery[36] or to hunt. And for everything else, they are very active and very cautious and skilful in everything that they want to do, reasoning very soundly over all that concerns them, hardworking for everything that can give them pleasure. They often endeavor to produce a large quantity of corn, beans, and other things which they sow as well. That is why they do not have any difficulty leaving their villages to go and wage war upon other nations, given that they leave to their families all that is necessary for their subsistence. That is the advantage that they have over some of the other nations in as much as they fall short of being as hardworking as the Iroquois. They

[f. 11r]
Sont aussi tres genereux et j'ay trouué en eux vne génerosité qui n'est point co͞mune aux autres sauuages, qui est l'hospitalité car quand ils rencontrent quelques françois ou autres qui manquent de viures ils se font vn vray plaisir de leur doñer le plus beau et meilleur qu'ils ont et le plus souuent ils arrêtent a leur Cabañes ceux qui y passent afin d'auoir tout le temps de les bien régaler.

De Leurs Qualitez

Si Cette Nation à quelques boñes qualités je leur en trouue de tres mauuaises je co͞menceray par l'yurognerie surquoy ils sont insatiables ce qui les rend capables de tout vice les fe͞mes ont cette passion co͞me les ho͞mes ce qui cause a cette nation bien du desordre qu'un ho͞me yure en poignarde vn autre qui ne le sera pas il en est quitte pour dire qu'il n'auoit point

<111>

are also very generous, and I have discovered a generosity in them that is not common to the other natives, which is hospitality. For when they encounter some Frenchmen or others who lack supplies, they take a real pleasure in giving them the very finest and best that they have. And most often they make those who pass by stop into their lodges, in order to have plenty of time to entertain them well.

Of Their Qualities

If this nation has some good qualities, I also find in them some very bad ones. I will begin with drunkenness, in which they are insatiable, and which renders them capable of every vice. The women have this passion like the men, which causes this nation a lot of havoc. If a drunk man were to stab another who is not drunk, he gets out of it by saying that he was out of his

[f. 11v]
d'esprit et que la boisson luy auoit ôteé la raison il est vray de dire que les familles interesseés tant d'une part que d'autre trauaillent a r'accom̄oder cette affaire et souuent le meurtrier se retire du village ap̄réhendant qu'il ne luy en soit fait autāt quand il leur arriue vn pàreil accident celuy qui est le meurtrier fait vn party de guerre a fin d'auoir vn prisoñier qu'il doñe a la place de celuy qu'il a tué et voila com̄e cela se r'accom̄ode et par la suite il se doñe bien de garde de se trouuer yure auec les parens de celuy dont il a esté le meurtrier veu que dans cette rencontre on pourroit le payer d'un même Coup ce qu'il n'ap̄réhende pas hors de la boisson qu'un de ces Sauuages saoül en trouue un autre qui ne le sera pas et qu'il luy dise je viens pour te tuër celuy qui n'a point beu baisse la tête et enfin attend auec vne patience inconceuable le Coup de la mort dont il est menacé ce qui

<IIV>

mind and that the drink had taken away his reason. It is true to say that the families, implicated as much on one side as on the other, may work to settle this affair; and often the murderer withdraws from the village fearing that much the same would be done to him. When a like accident happens to them, the one who is the murderer establishes a war party in order to take a prisoner, whom he presents in place of the one whom he has killed. And that is how the matter is resolved. And afterward he certainly guards himself against being found drunk with the relatives of the one whom he has murdered, seeing that in this encounter they could repay him with a like blow, which he does not fear without the drink. If one of these natives who is drunk were to find another of them who is not and were to say to him, "I am coming to kill you," the one who did not drink lowers his head and ultimately waits, with an inconceivable patience, for the death blow with which he is threatened, which

[f. 12r]

souuent arriue il ma arriué de pareilles auantures dans le temps que j'estois prisoñier chez les Sauuages j'êtois toûjours menacé de perdre la vie par ces sortes d'yurognes mais coñe je me tenois sur mes gardes et bien[8] resolu de me deffendre j'ay toujours crû que cela les retenoit et a empêche que je n'aye esté insulté d'eux.

De Leurs Superstitions

Tous les Sauuvages en general son superstiteux j'en remarque beaucoup dans cette nation coñe par exemple ils croyent ne deuoir jamais être atteints d'aucune maladie à moins qu'elle ne soit generale et toutes celles qui leur suruieñent en particulier ils les attribüent a quelque sort qu'on leur a jetté celuy donc qui en[9] est attaqué d'une a recours aussitôt au jongleur ou magicien et le prie de vouloir luy dire la cause de son indisposition & aussytôt ce faux deuin entre dans vne suërie ou il fait toutes sortes de contorsions hideu-

<12r>

often happens. Similar adventures happened to me during the time when I was a prisoner among the natives. I was always threatened with losing my life by these kinds of drunkards, but as I kept on my guard and remained well resolved to defend myself, I always believed that that held them back and prevented them from injuring me.

Of Their Superstitions

All of the natives in general are superstitious;[37] I notice a lot of it in this nation. For example, they believe that they ought never to be struck by any illness unless it be a general one. And all those sicknesses which happen to them in particular they attribute to some spell cast upon them. The one, then, who is attacked by one resorts immediately to the juggler[38] or magician and beseeches him kindly to tell him[39] the cause of his indisposition. And immediately this false soothsayer enters into a sweat lodge wherein he makes all sorts of hideous

[f. 12v]

ses et contrefait le cry de plusieurs sortes d'animaux et chante continuellement[10] et crie co͞me si on le battoit dans sa süerie enfin lassé de toutes ses folies il sort de sa suërie et dit au malade quil sçait celuy ou celle qui l'ont ensorcelé et les no͞me aussi-tôt les anciens ou guerriers de cette famille font uenir les accusés et leur demandent la raison pourquoy ils ont jetté de la mauuaise medecine sur vn tel et s'il s'en trouue qui n'ayent pas l'esprit de se deffendre ils sont assurés d'auoir la tête casseé et tout cela est causé par vne rancune de ce faux deuin qui est souuent cause de la ruine d'une famille entiere[11] Co͞me le propre de cette[12] est d'aimer beaucoup a faire la guerre souuent ils font des rêues a quoy ils ajoutent foy et pour se garentir d'un mauuais qu'ils croyent auoir fait ils font faire vn festin de dance de la maniere qu'ils le jugent a propos je dis cela ainsy attendu quils en ont de plusieurs sortes

<12v>

contortions and imitates the call of several kinds of animals and sings continuously and yells as if he were being beaten in his sweat lodge. Wearied, at last, by all his madness, he comes out of his sweat lodge and tells the one who is ill that he knows those, male or female, who have bewitched him, and he names them. Immediately, the elders or warriors of this family summon the accused and ask them the reason why they have cast bad medicine[40] on such a man. And if some of them are found not to have the wit to defend themselves, they are sure to have their skulls broken. And all that is caused by a grudge held by this false soothsayer, which is often the cause of an entire family's ruin, since the characteristic of this nation[41] is to be infatuated with waging war. They often have dreams in which they believe, and to protect themselves from a bad one that they believe they have had, they make a dance feast happen in the manner in which they deem it appropriate. I say that in this way, since they have several kinds of them.

[f. 13r]
celuy donc qui est prêt a partir pour la guerre demande a sa famille qu'il soit fait vn festin ou il ne doit auoir que des fem̃es qui y dansent auec chacune une tortüe a la main accom̃adeé exprés dans les quelles il y a quelques grains de rassade qui font du bruit a mesure qu'elles les remüent chacune des inuiteés y chante Sa chanson et y dansent toutes en rond auec des gestes qui Surpassent l'imagination et bien souuent à ces sortes de danses il y en a qui y sont toutes nües com̃e la main

De Leur Deüil

Il faut croire que cette nation est aussy sensible a la mort de leurs proches com̃e nous le som̃es des nôtres, le deüil de celuy qui a perdu son pere ou sa fem̃e est de s'ôter tous les bijoux qu'il a au Col ses pendans d'oreille et ses brasselets et cesse de s'accom̃oder la tête et ne paroît en aucune assembleé de diuertissemens se couure des

<13r>

The one, then, who is ready to depart for war asks his family to hold a feast for him at which only the women should dance, each with a turtle shell in hand, specially prepared, in which there are some beads[42] which make noise as the women shake them. Each one of the invited women sings her song, and they dance there all in a circle with gestures which surpass the imagination. And very often at these sorts of dances there are some women there who are completely naked, like the hand.

Of Their Mourning

One must believe that this nation is as moved by the death of their nearest ones as we are by that of ours. The grief of he who has lost his father or wife is expressed by casting off all the adornments[43] that he has around his neck, his earrings, and his bracelets. And he stops fixing his hair and does not appear at any entertaining gathering, and he covers himself in

[f. 13v]
plus mauuaises hardes qu'il ait, il cesse de porter ce deüil quand les plus proches parens du Côté de Son pere luy ordoñent de le quitter, ils en usent ainsy quand c'est pour une fem̃e;

La fem̃e qui a perdu son mary le porte plus triste que l'hom̃e elle quitte tous ses bijoux aussy et se ceinture d'une mauuaise couuerte, se couche sans se des'habiller a toûjours ses cheueux épars sur son corps et qui luy couurent tout le visage elle pleure presque toûjours cela continüe jusqu'a ce que les parens de son mary luy vieñent essuyer les larmes cela s'ap̃elle ôter le deüil. Cependant cette femme Continüe à pleurer soir et matin elle crie a pleine tête et autant de fem̃es qui se trouuent dans cette cabañe font la même chose toutes a la fois pendant l'espace d'une heure les guerriers qui sont en Cette Cabañe se trouuent tres

<13v>

the worst clothing that he may have. He stops grieving in this way when the nearest relatives on the side of his father order him to stop it. They treat it likewise when it is for a wife.

The wife who has lost her husband bears it with more sadness than the man. She also takes off all her adornments and girds herself with a wretched covering, goes to bed without undressing, and always lets her hair, which covers her whole face, hang down loose over her body. She is almost always weeping. That continues until the relatives of her husband come to wipe away her tears.[44] That is called "Removing the Mourning." In the meantime, this woman continues to weep morning and night. She cries out at the top of her voice, and as many women as are to be found in this lodge do the same thing, all at the same time for the space of an hour. The warriors who are in this lodge very

[f. 14r]
Souuent Sensibles à ces Sortes de pleurs ce qui les engagent d'ordinaire à partir pour la guerre pour venger cette mort Coṁe j'ay obmis cy deuant de vous parler de leur corporance je m'en uais en dire quelque chose je dis donc que les hommes sont bien proportioñés dans leur taille ils sont presque tous grand hoṁes ils ont l'air fort fier et sont assés alaigre de leur corps ils ne sont bazanés que parce qu'ils sont exposés presque tout nuds a l'ardeur du soleil ce qui contribüe encore beaucoup a leur rendre la peau noire sont les huiles et les graisses dont ils se frottent souuent le Corps ils n'ont point de barbe attendu qu'ils se l'arrachent a mesure qu'elle leur vient ils ont tous les cheueux noirs et fort longs les guerriers se les coupent du Côté droit a vn poulce de leur racine et laissent pendre ceux de la gauche

<14r>

often find themselves moved by these kinds of lamentation, which ordinarily commits them to leaving for war in order to avenge this death. As I have up until now omitted to speak to you about their physical appearance, I am going to say a few things about it. I say, then, that the men are well proportioned in their stature. They are nearly all tall men; they seem very proud and are lively enough in their bodies. They are tanned[45] only because they are exposed, almost completely naked, to the heat of the sun. What contribute even more to making their skin dark[46] are the oils and grease with which they often rub their bodies. They have no beard, given that they pluck it out as it comes in. They all have very long black hair. The warriors clip it on the right side within an inch[47] of its roots and allow that of the left to hang down.

[f. 14v]
les fem̃es et filles sont passablement jolies elles ont l'air fort doux la taille assés belle pendant qu'elles sont filles mais aussitôt qu'elles ont eües deux ou trois enfans elles deuieñent fort grosses elles sont fortes, vigoureuses, et tres peu sensibles au mal.

Il faut que je vous raconte ce que j'ay vû d'une de ces fem̃es la son mary étoit a la chasse a 12 ou 15 lieuës de son village cette fem̃e part pour l'aller joindre et luy porter des vivres et com̃e j'étois de sa famille elle me pria de faire ce voyage auec elle je le fis et a 8 lieuës du village cette fem̃e tombe malade pour accoucher elle me dit de passer outre et de luy aller faire du feu a vne cabane de l'autre côté d'une riuiere qu'il fallût passer gay dans l'eau jusqu'a la moitié des

<14v>

The women and girls are passably pretty. They seem very gentle and have a rather beautiful stature while they are girls, but as soon as they have had two or three children they become very fat. They are strong, robust, and not very susceptible to illness.

I must tell you what I saw of one of those women. Her husband was hunting twelve to fifteen leagues from his village. This woman sets out to go and join him and to carry supplies to him. And as I was of her family, she asked me to make this trip with her. I did so, and at eight leagues from the village this woman falls sick in childbirth. She tells me to carry on and go and make a fire for her at a lodge on the other side of a river that had to be forded[48] in water up to

[f. 151r]
cuisses je n'eus pas plus de temps qu'il m'en falloit pour allumer ce feu. enfin la feme arriue accouchée qu'elle estoit trauerse la riuiere dont jamais je ne fus plus surpris car il y auoit déja de la neige sur la terre donc il fasoit froid et aprés qu'elle se fût un peu chauffée elle prend son enfant le va lauer a la riuiere l'accomode a leur maniere ordinaire nous passons la la nuit et le lendmain nous passons et nous rendîmes ou êtoit son mary sans que cette sauuagesse eut le moindre accés de fiévre jugés de la si elles sont bien sensibles au mal.

<15r>

midthigh. I did not have any more time than was necessary for me to light this fire. Finally, the woman arrives, delivered of her child as she was, and crosses the river, by which I have never been more surprised, for there was already some snow on the ground, so that it was cold. And after she had warmed herself a little, she takes her child, goes to wash him in the river, and accommodates him in their usual fashion. We spend the night, and the next day we go on and betake ourselves to where her husband was, without this female native having the least attack of fever. Judge from that if those women are very susceptible to illness.

Appendixes

Appendix 1
Letter by Brigeac to Father Le Moyne

There are two of us prisoners from Montreal at Onneiout. Monsieur Vignal was killed by these Barbarians, having been unable to walk more than two days, because of his wounds. We arrived here on the first Sunday of December, in sad plight. My comrade has already had two finger-nails torn out. For the love of God, we pray you, repair hither and do your utmost, with presents, to rescue us and take us with you; and then we shall care no longer whether we die or not. We have made a compact to do and suffer all we can for the conversion of those who are killing us, and we pray to God daily for their salvation. We have not found a single Frenchman here, as we had hoped to do, and as would have greatly consoled us. I am writing you with my left hand.[1]

Your servant, Brigeac.

Appendix 2
Cruelties Practiced upon Some Frenchmen Captured by the Iroquois in the Year 1662

I give below a letter that has fallen into our hands concerning the cruel treatment which some Frenchmen received from the Iroquois two years ago, and of which we had not before learned.[1]

I make no change either in the wording or in the style of the letter, since its simplicity will, in the reader's mind, prove its chief claim to trustworthiness.[2]

On the 25th of the month of August, in the year 1662, fourteen Frenchmen were unexpectedly attacked by the Iroquois on a small Island near Montreal, and fled in disorder without offering much resistance.

Only Monsieur Brignac[3] *and two other Frenchmen, disregarding their comrades' flight, assumed an attitude of defense, and Monsieur Brignac killed the Captain of the Iroquois at the outset.*

The latter were immediately seized with fear and, seeing their Captain fallen, were already taking flight, when one of them began to harangue the others, saying to them: "Where, then, is our Nation's courage and renown? What ignominy for thirty-five warriors to flee before four Frenchmen!"

Meanwhile the other Frenchmen, who were in a boat, let themselves drift with the current and were exposed to all the enemy's shots, so that some were instantly killed, and others wounded.

At length, to return to the Iroquois, having recovered their courage, they came and fell upon the Frenchmen, mortally wounding an Ecclesiastic named Monsieur Vignal.

The two Frenchmen, their firearms being wet, were soon captured, together with Monsieur Brignac. The latter, however, made a stout resistance before letting himself be taken. Having his arm broken by a musket-shot, he still presented his pistol to the enemy; but, lacking strength to fire it, he plunged into the water, followed by the Iroquois, who caught him and dragged him over the rocks, head and face downward, around nearly the whole Island.

The Iroquois embarked with their prisoners, and all proceeded together to encamp at prairie d la Magdeleine, where they erected a fort; and, taking the body of Sieur Vignal, who was dead, the Iroquois stripped it and removed the flesh for eating.

As for the other two Frenchmen, who were uninjured, they were bound each to a tree; and as one of them, named René, was murmuring a prayer to God, a Savage who observed him asked him what he was doing, whereupon the Frenchman made answer that he was praying to God, and the Savage unbound him and said to him "Kneel down, and pray at thine ease."

Thus they passed the night in the fort which they had built; and on the next day, after eating the body of that good Priest and removing his scalp, pushed on to the Falls.

After this meal the Barbarians divided their forces, those of the Nation of Anniegué[4] *carrying off one Frenchman, whose name was du Fresne, and those of the Nation of Onneiout, who were much superior in numbers, leading away the two others.*

They proceeded eight days by land, René always laden like a packhorse, and most of the time entirely naked. Monsieur Brignac went along very quietly, scarcely able to walk because of the wounds on his head, feet, and whole body—which did not prevent him from ceaselessly praying to God.

After journeying for a week, the two bands which had separated reunited, and once more encamped together, loudly rejoicing and indulging in good cheer after their hunt.

Two among them went ahead, and carried the news to the villages.[5]

The Iroquois, perceiving that René had a psalter,[6] *and was reading therein, determined to cut off one of his thumbs, and forbade him to keep further company with Sieur Brignac, because they prayed together.*

Arriving at length at the village of the Nation of Onneiout, they stripped the two Frenchmen—Sieur Brignac and René—and painted their faces in native fashion. Then, after the enemy had arranged themselves for giving them the salute,—which consists in making the prisoners pass between two hedge-rows, so to speak, each person giving them a blow with a stick,—one of the elders cried out, "Enough, stop! Make way for them"; and, being conducted to the central space of this village, where a scaffold was prepared, they mounted it. Then an Iroquois took a stick, and struck René seven or eight blows with it, and plucked out his nails. After this, the two captives were made to come down, and were led into a cabin where the Council of the elders was in session.

The whole night was spent in making the two French prisoners sing, while to them was added an Algonquin captured from among the Outaouaks[7] *by another band.*

One of the cruelties exercised was the forcing of these three prisoners to exchange insults, and torture one another with coals of fire,—the Frenchmen being pitted against the Algonquin, and the Algonquin against the Frenchmen. But the latter would not obey such cruel orders, so that a Captain who saw that the Frenchmen were unwilling to harm the Algonquin, although they were maltreated by him, made them sit down near himself, as if to assure them of protection.

Finally, upon the Council's decreeing that the two Frenchmen should be burned, the sister of the Captain slain by Sieur Brignac said that she wished to have René to take the place of her dead brother. One of the old men declared this to be only fair, and it was granted, but not without opposition.

Sieur Brignac, however, was burned throughout the whole night, from his feet up to his waist, and on the next day these Barbarians still continued to burn him; but, after they had broken his fingers and had grown weary of burning him, one of their number stabbed him with a knife, tore out his heart, and ate it. They cut off his nose first, then his eyebrows, lips, and cheeks.

Throughout all that bloody and cruel execution, this poor Frenchman never ceased to entreat God for the conversion of these Barbarians, offering on their behalf all the agonies they made him suffer, and constantly saying: "I pray you, O God, to convert them; O God, convert them,"—ever repeating these words, and never crying out, however they might torture him.

Finally these Barbarians cut open his body and drank his blood—afterward cutting the body in pieces, putting these into a kettle, and eating them.

René received his freedom, but not without fears on his part; for, a sedition having arisen some time afterward, an Iroquois, holding a cocked pistol in his hand, entered the cabin where our Frenchman was, and asked him a question which greatly frightened him. He addressed him, as if he had said in our language, "Long live who—Father le Moyne or Father Chaumonot?" Then his adopted sister told the Frenchman to say, "Long live Father Chaumonot;" and so his life was saved on that occasion.

At length, after nineteen months of hardship and fatigue, encountered now in hunting, now in fishing, and again in an attack, which he had, of smallpox,—which swept away more than a thousand souls in the country of the Iroquois,—when he was out hunting young pigeons, in company with the Nations of Anniegué and Onneiout, it occurred to him to make his escape. Upon asking his comrade, du Fresne, who was with the people of Anniegué, whether he would run away, the latter told him no. Then, after devising a scheme with two other Frenchmen of the same village, when preparations for breaking up and returning home were in progress, he one evening asked one of the Iroquois in which direction the village lay, and in which one should go to reach the Dutch, and how many leagues distant they were. Being informed, he went and marked a tree, in order to remember the way he must take to reach them.

Indeed, when morning came, he noted the spot which he must pass in order to make his escape; and, while all were preparing to set out, each one loading himself with packages, the three Frenchmen took another route. Very fortunately, owing to a fire that some women had started among the leaves on the ground, causing them to be reduced to ashes or even to be dissipated, their footprints were not discovered.

They journeyed nine days before coming to New Holland, eating for their entire sustenance nothing but herbs which they found; for they had abandoned their packs in order to be more nimble for running. Nevertheless they were in great danger of recapture, and, as its necessary sequel, of being committed to the flames without hope of mercy.

They traveled only at night, and yet were constantly rushing, so to speak, into the enemy's hands, passing now inadvertently near the fishers' cabins, now near the hunters; again by day finding themselves in the immediate neighborhood of a village, and still again by night in the very midst of the cabins.

Four or five times they were pursued by the Iroquois, while on one occasion, among others, nearly all the youth of the second village of Anniegué started in pursuit of them. At other times, they were followed by warriors; and, still another time, by some men who were returning from trading with the Dutch.

After many dangers, they at last reached the country of the Dutch, but did not make themselves known until they ascertained whether any Iroquois were there. As there were none there at that time, they declared themselves to be Frenchmen and were received with open arms. They were conducted to the Governor of fort Orange,[8] *who received them very cordially, clothed them, and even freighted a shallop to convey them to Manhate, lest they might be discovered by the Iroquois and carried off.*

> *From Manhate they proceeded to Baston [Boston], and following all the coast as far as Quebec, they everywhere met with a kind reception. Thus ended happily their captivity, in which they were every day in danger of a cruel death.*

Such are the contents of the Letter, which does not tell half of the sufferings endured by those poor Frenchmen. Can the King's arms be better employed than in delivering us from the cruelty of those Barbarians?

Notes

Preface

1. "Nation Iroquoise," Bibiliothèque Mazarine, Paris, manuscrit 1964; "Nation Iroquoise," National Archives of Canada, Manuscript Group 7, IV, vol. 1964.
2. Bertrand, *Bibliothèque Sulpicienne*, 1:161; Leland, *Guide to Materials*, 266.
3. Roland Viau cited the document and, without comment, attributed it to the Jesuit Pierre Millet. Viau, *Enfants du néant*, 258.
4. Brandão, *"Your fyre shall burn no more,"* 19–30.
5. Gélinas, whose initials at the end of the brief introduction to the document indicate that he wrote the introduction, was particularly concerned by Boisvert's "ethnocentrism" and lack of professional objectivity. [Gélinas and Viau], "Nation Iroquoise," 31.
6. Boisvert, *Nation Iroquoise*, v–viii.
7. See note 3. It is not clear if Viau, who wrote the introduction to the special issue of *Recherches amérindiennes au québec* with Gélinas, did not accept Boisvert's conclusion about authorship or if he simply did not have time to revise his opinion between the time he read Boisvert's publication and the time his own book went into production.

The Iroquois and Their French Neighbors

1. Desrosiers, *Iroquoisie*, tome 1; Groulx, *Histoire du Canada français*.
2. Eccles, *French in North America*, 112; Brandão, *"Your fyre shall burn no more,"* 92–116.
3. Snow, *Iroquois*, 1–76.
4. Fenton, *Great Law and the Longhouse*, 24.
5. Brandão, *"Your fyre shall burn no more,"* 19–30.

6. Starna et al., "Northern Iroquoian Horticulture and Insect Infestation"; Starna and Relethford, "Deer Densities and Population Dynamics"; Fenton, "Northern Iroquoian Culture Patterns."
7. "Nation Iroquoise," f. 5v.
8. Lafitau, *Customs of the American Indians*, 1:287, 291; La Potherie, *Histoire de l'Amerique septentrionale*, 3:29; E. Tooker, "The League of the Iroquois: Its History, Politics, and Ritual," in Trigger, *Handbook of North American Indians*, 428.
9. Brandão, *"Your fyre shall burn no more"*; see especially figure 6.1 and the tables in appendix F.
10. Lafitau, *Customs of the American Indians*, 2:98. Recently it has been suggested that "slavery was practiced by Northern Iroquoians in the context of what has been previously and exclusively described as an adoption complex." Starna and Watkins, "Northern Iroquoian Slavery." Some prisoners were never fully adopted and were abused and made to perform menial tasks. These people may have been in some sort of "limbo" status until they could prove their worth as new "adoptees," or they may have been in this state on purpose to use in prisoner exchanges. Either way, this use of captives could only make capture of people more significant as a goal of warfare.
11. Bartram, *Observations on the Inhabitants*, 91. See also Anonymous, "Memoire sur les coutumes," 452.
12. [Ragueneau], *Relation of 1651–52*, in Thwaites, *Jesuit Relations and Allied Documents*, 38:49; [Le Mercier], *Relation of 1664–65*, 49:233 (hereafter *JR*).
13. See Trelease, *Indian Affairs in Colonial New York*.
14. Heidenreich, "Early French Exploration."
15. Moogk, *La Nouvelle France*, especially xv–xvi, 143–76; Eccles, "Social, Economic, and Political Significance."
16. By 1668 New France's population was just under eight thousand people. Moogk, *La Nouvelle France*, 105.
17. Heidenreich, "Early French Exploration."
18. Starna and Brandão, "From the Mohawk-Mahican War."
19. Starna and Brandão, "From the Mohawk-Mahican War"; Brandão, *"Your fyre shall burn no more,"* 95–102.

20. Brandão, *"Your fyre shall burn no more,"* appendix F, table F.2.
21. Brandão, *"Your fyre shall burn no more,"* 105–15.
22. Brandão, *"Your fyre shall burn no more,"* appendix F, table F.2.

Nation Iroquoise and Its Authorship

1. Seventeenth- and eighteenth-century French writers used a symbol, written like the number eight (8), to represent a sound in the Iroquoian languages that most closely resembles the *ou* sound in French. At times, as in "Nation Iroquoise," the "8" and *ou* were used interchangeably.
2. M. Pierre Gasnault, *conservateur en chef,* Bibliothèque Mazarine, to author, 20 mars, 1990. Boisvert (*Nation Iroquoise,* v) came to the same conclusion but does not indicate a source.
3. NAC, Manuscript Group 7, IV, 1964, p. 17. This version of the document is seventeen legal-sized pages long, written on one side only.
4. The thickness of the numbers was probably the result of pressing harder on the paper, or of writing more slowly, to make a small, neat number. Either practice would leave more ink on the paper.
5. I am indebted to Joseph L. Peyser and an anonymous reviewer for the University of Nebraska Press for this observation. The *conservateur en chef* at the Bibliothèque Mazarine, Monsieur Pierre Gasnault, dates the manuscript to the end of the seventeenth century, possibly to the eighteenth century, based on the orthography. Monsieur Pierre Gasnault to author, 20 mars 1990.
6. The same thing happened in 1931 when the document was transcribed for the National Archives of Canada. See the discussion in the section titled "Notes on Transcription and Translation."
7. The numbers in parentheses in this paragraph refer to folio numbers in the document.
8. Brandão, *"Your fyre shall burn no more,"* graph 7.1.
9. For a list of those captured by the Iroquois before 1666 and their eventual fates, see Dickinson, "La guerre iroquoise," 48–53.
10. Campeau, *Monumenta Novae Franciae*; Thwaites, *Jesuit Relations and Allied Documents.* On the relative merits of the two series, see Codignola, "Battle Is Over."

11. Thwaites had done a fairly comprehensive job of compiling material for his series, and Father Campeau's work is even more thorough. The latter has combed the various archives in Rome and Europe for Jesuit material. Father Campeau recalls finding "Nation Iroquoise" only at the Bibliothèque Mazarine. Father Lucien Campeau, S.J., to author, 18 avril 1991.
12. Lucien Campeau, "Pierre Millet," in Brown et al., *Dictionary of Canadian Biography*, 2:473–74 (hereafter, DCB).
13. Father Millet in [Dablon], *Relation of 1673–74*, in Thwaites, JR, 58:185–89.
14. Monsieur Louis Tronson, the Sulpician superior in Paris, often admonished the Canadian priests to be on good behavior with the Jesuits. Monsieur Tronson a Monsieur Lefevre, 5 avril 1677, in Bertrand, *Correspondance de M. Louis Tronson*, 2:140; Monsieur Tronson a Monsieur de Belmont, 6 juin 1682, 2:247–48. On the not always coordinated efforts of the early missionaries, see Codignola, "Competing Networks," 539–84.
15. Father Lucien Campeau, S.J., to author, 18 avril 1991. Boisvert (*Nation Iroquoise*, vii) also concluded that a Jesuit could not have written "Nation Iroquoise."
16. Dollier de Casson, *History of Montreal*; [de Galinée], "Ce que s'est passé"; Belmont Vachon, *Histoire du Canada*.
17. Bertrand, *Correspondance de M. Tronson*; Bertrand, *Bibliothèque sulpicienne*; Migne, *Oeuvres complète de M. Tronson*.
18. Bertrand, *Correspondance de M. Tronson*, 1:161.
19. See, for example, Monsieur Tronson a Monsieur Mariel, 23 avril 1678, in Bertrand, *Correspondance de M. Tronson*, 2:170–71; Monsieur Tronson a Monsieur de Belmont, 15 avril 1685, 2:278. One historian of the Sulpicians has suggested that Monsieur Tronson asked for annual relations and that the priests complied. If so, they have been lost to posterity. Maurault, *La Compagnie de Saint-Sulpice*, 5. Possibly they were destroyed along with Sulpician letters during the French Revolution. Preston and Lamontagne, *Royal Fort Frontenac*, 6 n. 4.
20. Aumont, *Les Prêtres de Saint-Sulpice*.
21. Baugy, *Journal d'une expédition*; Boucher, *Histoire véritable et naturelle*;

[Guyart], *Marie de L'Incarnation, Ursuline*; Lafitau, *Customs of the American Indians*; Lahontan, *New Voyages to North America*; La Potherie, *Histoire de L'Amerique septentrionale*; Perrot, *Memoire sur les moeurs*; [Radisson], *Explorations of Pierre Esprit Radisson*; Sagard, *Long Journey to the Country*; Sagard, *Histoire du Canada*.

22. Jamet, *Les annales de l'Hotel-Dieu*; anonymous, "Memoire sur les coutumes"; Le Blant and Baudry, *Nouveau Documents sur Champlain*; Margry, *Découvertes et établissements*; Margry, *Relations et mémoires inédits*; [Morin], *Histoire simple et véritable*; *Rapporte de L'archiviste de la province de Quebec*.
23. [Raudot], *Relation*.
24. Boisvert came to the same conclusion and published letters from Raudot's work based upon "Nation Iroquoise." Boisvert, *Nation Iroquoise*, 52–62.
25. Rochemontiex's version of Raudot's *Relation* has been translated and published. See Silvy, *Letters from North America*. The erroneous attribution of Raudot's *Relation* to Father Antoine Silvy, made when Rochemontiex first published the work, is repeated and reinforced by Dickson. When Father Rochemonteix published the manuscript in 1904 he argued that it was written by Father Silvy, but Rochemontiex did not list him as the author on the cover. By 1939 it was clear that Raudot was the author of the *Relation*. On this matter, see the discussion later in this chapter.
26. The following examples are offered in French to avoid the question of whether or not the similarities are the result of the translation process. A translation is offered in the notes. To facilitate reference checks, and because the passages from Raudot's unpublished manuscript are identical in Rochemontiex's published edition, references to Raudot's work are to the latter.
27. [Raudot], *Relation*, 185.
28. "Nation Iroquoise," f. 4v. "He then, or she, who has some propositions to make begins by assembling the elders of his or her family, and if it is something that concerns the warriors, one or two captains of this same family group are summoned to be witnesses to the thing being proposed." The change Raudot introduced in this passage

bears comment. The author of "Nation Iroquoise" clearly meant to state that men or women could initiate councils. As Raudot edited this passage, he left women out of this process.

29. [Raudot], *Relation*, 193.
30. "Nation Iroquoise," f. 3r. "The religion of these peoples consists of very few things. They do not recognize any other God than the Sun, and it is to it that they address themselves in all their needs, as much for war as for the hunt. That is why they never undertake anything without first having offered smoke to this heavenly body."
31. Donald J. Horton, "Antoine-Denis Raudot," in Brown, *DCB*, 2:549–54.
32. Rochemonteix, introduction, xxviii, xii.
33. Rochemonteix, introduction,, xii–xiii.
34. See Delanglez, *Frontenac and the Jesuits*, 65 n. 44.
35. Archives Nationales, Archives des Colonies, Series C11A, 122 (hereafter, AN, C11A).
36. Yves Zoltvany, "Louis La Porte de Louvigny," in Brown, *DCB*, 2:345–47.
37. For Margry's note see AN, C11A, 122: n.p., but following letter 90 of "Suitte de la relation par lettres de l'Amerique septentrionalle."
38. Kinietz, *Indians of the Western Great Lakes*, 336.
39. On de Liette and the sources of his writings, in translation, see C. J. Russ, "Pierre-Charles di Liette," in Brown, *DCB*, 2:435–36.
40. Note, 24 sept. 1709, Correspondance Raudot-Pontchartrain, AN, C11G, 4:242v. It is not clear from the references in their respective works that Delanglez and Kinietz ever saw this note. Both seem to have taken Margry on his authority in this matter.
41. See, for example, Champigny et Frontenac au ministre, 9 nov. 1694, AN, C11A, 13:296–313; Vaudreuil au ministre, 14 nov. 1713, 34:45–54.
42. Roy, *La famille de La Porte de Louvigny*, 12. On the peace settlement, see Brandão and Starna, "Treaties of 1701."
43. La Potherie au ministre, 16 oct. 1700, AN, C11A, 18:156.
44. Roy, La *famille de La Porte de Louvigny*, 5, 8–9.
45. Roy, La *famille de La Porte de Louvigny*, 37–38.
46. Roy, La *famille de La Porte de Louvigny*, 7, 10.

47. Roy, *La famille de La Porte de Louvigny,* 13–17.
48. Roy, *La famille de La Porte de Louvigny.*
49. Brandão, *"Your fyre shall burn no more,"* appendix D.
50. Brandão, *"Your fyre shall burn no more,"* appendix D and chapter 4. For the names, fates, and location of captives taken by the Iroquois before 1666, see Dickinson, "La guerre iroquoise," 51–53.
51. Father Lucien Campeau first suggested Le Moyne as the possible author of "Nation Iroquoise" in a 1991 letter to me.
52. Jean-Jacques Lefebvre, "Charles Le Moyne de Longueuil et Châteauguay," in Brown, *DCB,* 1:463–65; Belmont, *Histoire,* 4–8; Dollier de Casson, *Histoire,* 201, 203.
53. Faillon, *Histoire de la colonie française,* 3:108.
54. Faillon, *Histoire de la colonie française,* 3:108; Dollier de Casson, *Histoire,* 299, 301; Traite de Paix demandée par six ambassadeurs Iroquois . . . [dec. 1665], AN, C11A, 2:187–90v. Dollier de Casson places the capture in July and Faillon in August. Faillon remarked that Le Moyne was returned within three months, thus in November. The Traite de Paix . . . , which dates from December, notes that Le Moyne had been released as a sign of Iroquois respect for the French, but it is not clear if Le Moyne was returned earlier or at the time of the conference. He was most likely returned at the time of the conference to assure protection against French reprisal upon Iroquois peace delegates and for the opportunity to make the grand gesture of his return at the conference.
55. Dollier de Casson, *Histoire,* 299, 301. This was the army that accompanied the newly arrived lieutenant-general of French America, Alexandre de Prouville de Tracy.
56. Claude Perrault, "René Cuillerier," in Brown, *DCB,* 2:164–65; Jaenen, *Role of the Church,* 8–9.
57. Perrault, "René Cuillerier," in Brown, *DCB,* 2:164–65.
58. The information in the rest of the paragraph is based on two reports of the event: one by Brigeac and the other by an unidentified person who could only have been Cuillerier. See Lalemant, *Relation of 1661–62,* in Thwaites, *JR,* 47:177–79; [Le Mercier], *Relation of 1664–65,* 50:55–67. Transcripts of these documents can be found in appen-

dixes 1 and 2. See also Dollier de Casson, *Histoire*, 283–85. For Cuillerier as the source of the captivity narrative in the *Relation of 1664–65*, see the discussion in the text.

59. [Le Mercier], *Relation of 1664–65*, in Thwaites, *JR*, 50:55–67. The account here dates the initial attack as being on 25 August, 1662. Other sources, including a letter written by Brigeac from captivity, make it clear that the attack took place in 1661. See [Le Jeune], *Relation of 1661–62*, 47:177–79.

60. Cuillerier's literacy level is uncertain. A minority of people in the colony were able to sign their names, and Cuillerier was among those, but to what extent he could write is unclear. See Claude Perrault, "René Cuillerier," in Brown, *DCB*, 2:164–65; Greer, *People of New France*, 46). I am indebted to Joseph L. Peyser for copies of notarial documents with Cuillerier's signature.

61. Brandão, "*Your fyre shall burn no more*," appendix D, raids from October 1661 to May 1663. Dickinson ("La guerre iroquoise," 53), lists eight French taken captive for this same period.

62. [Le Mercier], *Relation of 1664–65*, in Thwaites, *JR*, 50:63.

63. "Nation Iroquoise," 11v–12r.

64. Boisvert mentions Michel Messier as another possible candidate for author of "Nation Iroquoise" but dismisses the probability because Messier was captured twice. Boisvert finds it hard to credit, and rightly so, that Messier would not mention such a significant occurrence in his story. Boisvert, *Nation Iroquoise*, vii. It also appears that Messier was first captured by the Mohawks and then possibly by the Onondagas. The circumstances surrounding his captivity and release or escape are murky. See Claude Perrault, "Michel Messier," in Brown, *DCB*, 2:469–70.

65. Boisvert (*Nation Iroquoise*, viii) does not think that Cuillerier wrote the document shortly after his return to New France because he did not want anyone feeling sorry for his situation. Boisvert offers no reason or evidence in support of this assessment.

66. See Brandão, "*Your fyre shall burn no more*," appendix D, raid dated 25 Oct. 1661 and the sources listed there. See also [Le Jeune], *Relation of 1661–62*, in Thwaites, *JR*, 47:175–79.

67. [Le Mercier], *Relation of 1664–65*, in Thwaites, *JR*, 50:65–67.
68. An entry in the *Journal des Pères Jésuites, 1663*, dated 30 July, recorded the arrival at Quebec of an English bark with seven Frenchmen "saved from the yroquois." In Thwaites, JR, 47:305–7. Cuillerier may have been among those men.
69. In 1664 the last ship sailed for France on 23 Sept. *Journal des Pères Jésuites, 1664*, in Thwaites, *JR*, 48:239.
70. By the 1600s the categories that writers who examined different cultures were expected to cover were well established. Some dated back to the age of Herodotus. Hodgen, *Early Anthropology*, 23, 167–68.
71. On Jesuit conversion processes see Axtell, *Invasion Within*.
72. [De Galinée], "Ce que s'est passé." The Sulpicians were conscious of the need to record their work, as did the Jesuits. In 1688 their Paris-based superior, Monsieur Tronson, admonished them to prepare *mémoires* with an eye to publication. It is probably in compliance with that request that Dollier de Casson and François de Belmont, Canadian superiors of the order, wrote their respective histories of Montreal and Canada. Monsieur Tronson a Monsieur de Belmont, avril 1688, in Bertrand, *Correspondance de M. Tronson*, 2:293–94.
73. Gordon M. Sayre has examined a wide array of French-language literature relating to the early colonial period and found that most of that material can be divided into two groups: *récits de voyage* (travel writings) or *moeurs des sauvages* (ethnographic descriptions). Sayre, *Les Sauvages américains*, 24. Cuillerier's *mémoire*, although unpublished for centuries, clearly belongs in the latter category.
74. Of course, Cuillerier emphasized what he found interesting, and he made observations that are not always found elsewhere, such as the reference to worshipping the sun.
75. Richter, "Ordeals of the Longhouse," 11–27; Fenton, *Great Law and the Longhouse*. For a dissenting view see Deer, "La 'loi des condoléance,'" 65–66.
76. Lafitau, *Customs of the American Indians*, 1:293.
77. It is possible to argue that this practice of honorary titles dates back to at least the 1640s and that the League/Confederacy was functioning then. In the 1640s the Mohawks met with French governor Mont-

magny, whose name they translated as Onontio, or "Large Mountain." This is a literal rendering of the French governor's name. It is clear that the Mohawks and other Iroquois viewed this name as an honorary title, such as they had among themselves in the League, because they continued to use the term Onontio to describe the Frenchman who occupied the office of governor long after Montmagny was dead.

78. An anonymous, and often cited, description of the Iroquois clan system usually dated to 1666 is the most detailed early account of one aspect of Iroquois society. See La Nation Iroquois . . . , AN, C11A, 2:264–67. This, too, is a scribe's copy. The handwriting is different from that in "Nation Iroquoise," and unlike the copyist of "Nation Iroquoise," that of La Nation wrote out the double consonant. The scribe for "Nation Iroquoise" wrote only one consonant and placed a symbol over top of it to signify a double consonant. A translation of La Nation is to be found in O'Callaghan, *Documents Relative to the Colonial History*, 9:47–51. Roland Viau, again without comment, has attributed this document to the Jesuit Father Pierre-Joseph-Marie Chaumonot. Viau, *Enfants du néant*, 96, 258.

Notes on Transcription and Translation

1. Raudot recognized these limitations in the manuscript from which he worked, and the major difference between "Nation Iroquoise" and the abbreviated portions of it in Raudot's *Relation* is that Raudot tidied up the syntax and grammar.
2. On the problems presented in translating this type of document and of striking a balance between "readability" and maintaining "authorial voice," see Peyser, *On the Eve of the Conquest*, 43–45.
3. Raudot, "Relation," AN, C11A, 122: lettre 76e.

Nation Iroquoise

1. The word *vilage* was written, in smaller print, in the margin. It may have been omitted by the person telling the story or later during the writing or copying process. The word was then added for clarity or to

correct an oversight. *Vilage* is written in the same hand as the rest of the text.

2. The capital letter *E* is written over the lowercase *e* in this word.
3. Boisvert (*Nation Iroquoise,* 3) adds *sortes* just before this word and claims, without citing a page reference, to follow Rochemontiex in this practice (24). Boisvert may be correct that a word is needed here (the French reads better with this word in place), but neither Rochemontiex in his edited version of Raudot's work nor Raudot in the original included this portion on birds from "Nation Iroquoise." See the published *Relation* at page 196 and the manuscript version at lettre 81e.
4. The flourish that the writer usually adds after a subject heading is missing in the following heading and after the section titled *Conseils Pour aller Pleurer Les Morts* (f. 91). In the latter instance the heading is at the end of the page, and there is no room for the symbol. In the following heading the writer seems to have forgotten to add it.
5. Here a word is blotted out, and the word *Des* is written in above it.
6. There is an *e* missing in the word *tout* and a *t* missing from *veulen* in the following line. Both letters are needed for grammatical reasons.
7. The grammatically correct spelling for this word is *concerne.* The word needs to agree with the *qui les* preceding it and thus should be singular.
8. There is a word blotted out here between *bien* and *resolu.* It looks as if the writer sought to add the word *resolu* at the end of the line near the right-hand margin of the folio sheet. Then, realizing that there was not enough space, he crossed out what he had begun, and put the word on the next line at the left-hand margin.
9. The word *en* was written in above the *que* and *est.* It was obviously left out and written in afterward.
10. Between the words *continuellement* and *et* another word has been crossed out. It appears to be the word *comme,* with the usual practice of a single, rather than double, consonant.
11. The last letter in the word *entiere* (the *e*) is written in above the word. The writer ran out of space on the right-hand side of the folio sheet.
12. There appears to be a word missing here. The word *cette* needs some-

thing to which to refer, and it is clear from the sentence that the reference is to the Iroquois and not to *famille* in the proceeding line. Boisvert added *nation* in the place of the missing word. Boisvert, *Nation Iroquoise*, 15.

The Iroquois Nation

1. In the early 1660s the Iroquois League was made up of five nations (Mohawks, Oneidas, Onondagas, Cayugas, and Senecas) and thus of five areas of village concentration. However, there were more than five villages. The author appears to be using *village* to mean what today could be called a "group" or "tribe." *Village* here, and in the next lines in the text, should be read to mean "village area" or "groups." For the locations of the major Iroquois villages see the map included in this volume.

   It is difficult to translate these terms effectively. They are, in fact, the proper names, in French, of the various Iroquois nations and people. The English equivalents are Mohawks, Oneidas, Onondagas, Cayugas, and Senecas. If one reads the term *villages* preceding these names to mean "groups," as was likely intended, then the names can be rendered as Mohawks, Oneidas, etc. But if one reads *villages* to mean "village areas," then *Agnez*, *Oney8t*, etc., are being used, incorrectly, as proper names for the villages or areas where the villages were located even though, as the author must have known, the villages had names that differed from those of the nations. The French often referred to the large area the Iroquois inhabited as *Iroquoisie,* which is translated as "Iroquoia." Limited by the language of his day and with no accepted term to describe the individual tribal homelands, the author was likely attempting to do something similar with the names for each tribal area. Jesuit missionaries initially used the same tactic in their correspondence and later distinguished between the place and its people by adopting an Iroquoian suffix that meant "people of." The Jesuits and later French writers were thus able to distinguish between *Agnier* (Mohawk territory) and *Agnieronons* (Mohawk peoples). But although *Iroquoisie* can be translated as "Iroquoia," no such English equivalents exist for the individual tribal areas. The best that can be done is some stilted expression such as "Mohawkia" or "Senecaia," or the cumbersome "Mohawk territory." The latter expression would be nonsensical or would require major changes in the author's prose. For example, "the first village, which is Mohawk territory, is close to . . . ," or "the first group of people are the Mohawks, who are close to . . . ." For all of the above reasons, each designation implies both a placename and a national group, here and in the next few sentences, without further specification.

Fort Orange, the Dutch trading post on the Hudson River founded in 1624, was renamed Albany after the English takeover of the colony in 1664.

2. The French *league*, as a unit of linear measurement in this period, roughly equaled three statute miles. Heidenreich, *Huronia*, 23; Trudel, *Le débuts du régime seigneurial*, xxi.

3. It is virtually impossible to assess the accuracy of the author's figures because we do not know which village in each nation marked his beginning or end destination, nor which routes he took. Comparisons with other estimates by other observers are subject to the same difficulties; however, the author's estimates appear to be within the range of distances others noted. Compare his estimates with those of Raudot, "Relation," AN, C11A, 122: lettre 75e, and the Jesuits Father François Le Mercier ([Le Mercier], *Relation of 1664–65*, in Thwaites, *JR*, 49:257–59) and Father Vincent Bigot ([Bigot], *Relation of 1679*, *JR*, 61:165). Father Claude Dablon also edited this relation but left Bigot's estimates untouched (see table 1).

Table 1. *Estimated Distance between Iroquois Nations*

Nation	*"Nat Iroq"*	*Le Mercier*	*Bigot*	*Raudot*
Mohawks-Oneidas	25 L	45 L	35 L	no data
Oneidas-Onondagas	18 L	15 L	10 L	16 L
Onondagas-Cayugas	20 L	23–30 L	17 L	16 L
Cayugas-Senecas	12 L	no data	25 L	11 L

The Jesuit Father Jacques Bruyas, who worked among the Oneidas, put the distance from the Mohawks to the Oneidas at thirty leagues. Letter from Reverend Father Jacques Bruyas, 21 Jan. 1668, in Thwaites, *JR*, 51:121.

The estimate by the author of "Nation Iroquoise" of the total span of Iroquois village area, 75 leagues, works out to approximately 225 miles. The distance, by air, from the Genesee River to the junction of the Mohawk River and Scoharie Creek, the western and eastern limits of Iroquois village sites around 1660, is about 180–200 miles. Father Le Mercier thought Iroquois territory spanned 100 to 150 leagues. [Le Mercier], *Relation of 1664–65*, in Thwaites, *JR*, 49:257–59. Raudot put the distance at 70 Leagues ("Relation," AN, C11A, 122: lettre 75e). The latter, despite his reliance on "Nation Iroquoise" for much of his information on the Iroquois, clearly derived his distance estimates from a different source.

4. The description and assessment of the quality of flora and fauna in Iroquoia that follows is echoed by other French observers who visited the area at about the same time. See [Le Mercier], *Relation of 1664–65*, in Thwaites, *JR*, 49:259; Letter from Reverend Father Jacques Bruyas, 21 Jan. 1668, 51: 121–23; [Le Jeune], *Relation of 1656–57*, 43:257–61.
5. The author used *sauvage*, which translates as "savage," when referring to Indians. However, a literal translation of *sauvage* seems inappropriate, given the loaded meaning its English equivalent has taken on. The French term had no pejorative meaning most of the time and is best rendered as "Native." When French writers wanted to pass moral judgment on Natives they tended to use the French term for "barbarians" (*barbares*).
6. The author's meaning is not clear. The French term he used here, *affranchir*, means "to set free." Transplanting a vine to another place might fit this meaning, as might the notion of pruning the vine to "free" it of needless growth. Either reading of the word would make sense here. Aurélien Boisvert (*Nation Iroquoise*, 21, n. 19) defines *affranchir* in horticultural terms as *greffer au pied* (graft at the base).
7. A check through a number of Middle French and historical French Canadian dictionaries failed to turn up any such word that referred

to a fruit. Nor was Boisvert able to locate the term in specialized flora catalogues. Boisvert, *Nation Iroquoise*, 22, n. 20. *Darille* may have been a term specific to the region of France from whence the author hailed.

8. The author wrote *Rats de bois* here. It is not clear if the expression was intended as a noun or as a description, and the term does not show up in seventeenth- and eighteenth-century French dictionaries. It is most likely that the author was referring to the North American opossum. Writing in 1699, the Jesuit Julien Binneteau remarked upon a *rat de bois*, the female of which "carries her young in a sort of pouch under her belly" (in Thwaites, *JR*, 65:72, 73). Grimm's *Deutsches Wörterbuch* (vol. 27:1180) lists *rat de bois* under *Waldratte* (opossum). My thanks to Corinna Dally-Starna for the latter reference.
9. The starling, common in France, was not introduced into North America until the 1890s. What the author saw was, apparently, a small iridescent black flock bird. He may have seen the common grackle or the rusty blackbird. Both species fit the general description of the starling.
10. "Kinds" (*sortes*) is supplied here as logic suggests is needed.
11. There is a certain ambiguity in the French when referring to the sun. That ambiguity is best maintained, and the English made more readable, by referring to the sun consistently as "it." Ivy Dickson, when translating this passage in Raudot, came to a similar resolution to this problem. Silvy, *Letters from North America*, letter 80.
12. The French past participle *atteints* meant *convaincus* in the sixteenth and seventeenth centuries. Huguet, *Dictionnaire de la langue française*. Middle English cognates are linked to the Act of Attainder (1459), which itself derived from the French past participle *attaint* (cited first in 1303, *Oxford English Dictionary*) meaning "convicted."
13. The author may have meant "clan" or "clan lineage" when he referred to *famille*. However, the term *clan* entered the French language only around 1740 and took on its current anthropological meaning around 1800. Adopting a literal translation here prevents the introduction of an anachronism into the text.

14. The French word *faits*, translated here as "procedure," implies more than "facts" or "events"; i.e., "the course of events," glossed by Boisvert as *"la conduite à tenir."* Boisvert, *Nation Iroquoise*, 30, n. 69).
15. What the author writes reveals familiarity with an Iroquois concept. At council meetings strings and belts of wampum (small beads made from shells and later of glass) were draped on a string strung between two sticks stuck in the ground. Sometimes they were placed on a mat laid in the center of the council circle. To put a proposition on the mat was a metaphor meaning to bring it up for discussion. On the process of Iroquois councils in the seventeenth century and metaphors used there, see Jennings, *History and Culture of Iroquois Diplomacy*. On wampum and its uses, see Vachon, "Colliers et ceintures de porcelaine dans la diplomatie indienne"; Vachon, "Colliers et ceintures de porcelaine chez les indiens"; Michael K. Foster, "Another Look at the Function of Wampum in Iroquois-White Councils," in Jennings, *History and Culture of Iroquois Diplomacy*, 99–114.
16. "Wampum" is supplied here. The author used *collier*, which really means "necklace," to refer to strings beaded with wampum. The meaning would have been clear to readers familiar with Native diplomacy, since all *colliers* and *ceintures* (belts) used in diplomacy were made of wampum. See sources cited in note 15. However, it seemed necessary to provide the extra word in order to have the English accurately reflect the intent of the French.
17. *Villages* here could be read to mean the other villages of a nation, or it might refer to the other nations of the League.
18. The author is referring to the three clans of the Oneidas.
19. That is, the one chosen as speaker for the principal war chiefs.
20. Other authorities describe this pre-battle meeting as a type of feast, and the kettle was used to prepare food to serve to those about to go to war. See, for example, Lafitau, *Customs of the American Indians*, 2: 111–12; Boucher, *Histoire véritable et naturelle*, 119. This event was so firmly a part of the ritual of war that to "put the kettle to boil" was a euphemism for war and to "knock over the kettle" meant that war was being averted.
21. The author probably meant that the elder announced the results of

the war council to the village and urged people to begin war preparations, rather than the elder raised a cry of alarm.

22. The form *leurs* must be an error for *les* here, since *leur* (to them) makes no sense and, as an indirect object, cannot be inflected with a plural *s*. Finally, the verb for "carry" requires a direct, not an indirect, object in this context.
23. The parallel construction of *ou ils* (twice) makes "and" a good alternative for avoiding the repetition of which English is less tolerant.
24. In using *a* (*à*, interpreted here as a dative of purpose) the author is drawing a ratio comparison.
25. "Taken" is used here to mean "conquered."
26. He probably meant that the captives were divided up among the various Iroquois nations.
27. *Feu* (fire) is used as a synonym for torture, which most often involved using fire. On Iroquois torture practices see Knowles, "Torture of Captives by the Indians."
28. The use of "revenge" (*vengeance*) here suggests that the person lost was killed in battle. The same process, as the author makes clear a few sentences later on, was followed to capture people to replace those lost due to illness or natural death.
29. "Wampum" is supplied here. See note 16.
30. *Saluade* (greeting) is clearly not an Iroquois word. The author most likely meant that it was an Iroquois expression to call the process of beating a prisoner a "greeting."
31. The expression *pour lors* meant "in this case" in 1688 (*Trésor de la langue française,* 10:1369b).
32. The French word here, *porcelaine* (porcelain), was the accepted way to refer to what, in English, is known as wampum.
33. Normally *faire une perte* would be translated by "cause the ruin" or, in this context, "the ruin they have caused," but this is clearly not the meaning intended here. The sense of the statement is that the grieving side thanks the visitors for coming to console them in their time of mourning.
34. *Villages* here should be read to mean "nations."
35. He probably meant "and that has appeared in many ways," but that is not exactly what is written in French.

36. Given the context, one assumes that "discovery" means to gather intelligence.
37. It is worth noting that the author distinguished between Iroquois religion and what he considered "superstitions." Many early writers did not and lumped the two together—usually as superstitions. Modern students of the Iroquois tend to speak of an Iroquois world-view or cosmology. This approach takes into account all of the various ways by which the Iroquois tried to explain, order, and deal with the seen and unseen forces in the world around them. Snow, *Iroquois*.
38. The French word that is translated here as "juggler" (*jongleur*) has deep historical connotations for the French. The statutes from an early-fourteenth-century confraternity of *jongleurs* in Paris, for example, use the terms *menestreurs* and *menestrelles* (male and female minstrels) as synonyms. Cf. Faral, *Les jongleurs en France*, 128–30, and Page, *Owl and the Nightingale*, 204–5. In the sixteenth century *jongleur* meant "juggler" or, more broadly, "entertainer," with pejorative connotations of deceit. In the new world the same term was applied to the "shaman" who, from the European perspective, manipulated the Natives into believing in their powers of divination. French missionaries, in particular, considered Native shamans to be either frauds or Satan's henchmen. (Recently, however, Peter A. Goddard has argued that modern scholars have misread much of the missionaries' writings regarding demons. Goddard, "Devil in New France.") The pejorative sense of *jongleur*, applied by early French-Canadian writers in general, likened the histrionic aspect of the curing ritual to trickery or entertainment.
39. Iroquois society worked on a consensual basis. Especially when dealing with the spirit world, coercion was not acceptable and could hardly be efficacious. The author's phrasing, *le prie de vouloir luy dire*, suggests that, despite his disbelief in shamanistic power, he had picked up on the Iroquois practice of appealing to the "good nature" of the shaman so that the latter acted not because he had been asked but out of his desire to be generous.
40. "Evil or bad spell" might make more sense here, but *medecine* does not mean "spell." The author has just used the word *sort* for "spell"

and therefore has deliberately chosen not to use it here. His choice of French words here may, again, have reflected his attempt to translate words or concepts from Iroquois language and culture.

41. The word *nation* is missing in the French text. The missing word must be both singular and feminine. "Nation" seems the likeliest possibility.
42. *Grains de rassade* refer to beads of glass or porcelain used specifically in Native trade. Glass beads came to replace Native wampum in many areas, and the author might have meant that wampum was put in the rattles.
43. *Bijoux* means "jewelry," but the Iroquois did not have jewels in the literal sense. They did, however, adorn themselves with a variety of decorative objects made from all sorts of material. "Adornments" seems to best convey what those objects were and what they meant.
44. This seems to be, as is the following statement, a fairly literal rendering of a specific Iroquois expression.
45. *Bazané* refers to the process of tanning hides or the color of a tanned hide. Here the author must have meant the "dark" color of a tanned hide, since he goes on to say that the Iroquois are dark because they get tanned by the sun.
46. *Noire* means "black" but can be used to imply "darkness."
47. *Poulce* (*pouce* in modern French) means "thumb." A "thumb" was also a unit of measure roughly equal to one inch.
48. *Passer gay* is really *passer à gué*, which means to "ford."

Appendix 1

This translation is taken from Lalemant's *Relation of 1661–62*, in Thwaites, *JR* 47:177–79. Father Le Moyne, as Brigeac knew, was stationed among the Onondagas.

1. Brigeac had his right arm broken during the capture. Lalemant's *Relation of 1661–62*, in Thwaites, *JR* 47:177–79.

Appendix 2

This translation is taken from Le Mercier's *Relation of 1664–65*, in Thwaites, *JR* 50:55–67. As discussed earlier, the dates given in this document, in the title and in the letter, are off by one year.

1. Either Le Mercier, the author of this *Relation*, forgot the letter about this event in Lalement's *Relation* of 1661, or he meant that a full account of what had happened to the captives was unknown.
2. The letter that follows is clearly written either in the third-person narrative voice by someone who was party to the events described or by someone not party to the events but who based the letter on the account of an eyewitness—probably the latter. Given that René Cuillerier is mentioned directly, and that the letter recounts his personal trials and other events from his perspective, it can only have been based on his testimony.
3. This is an obvious misspelling of Brigeac.
4. The Mohawks.
5. Compare the description here of what René Cuillerier saw and suffered as a war prisoner with the description of the process described by the author of "Nation Iroquoise."
6. A small book of Psalms used for devotional purposes.
7. The Ottawas, an Algonquian-speaking group.
8. Present-day Albany, New York. "Manhate," in this same sentence, is a reference to Manhattan.

Bibliography

Archival Sources

Archives Nationales (AN), Paris, Archives des Colonies, Series C11A, Correspondance General, Canada, and Series C11G, Correspondance Raudot-Pontchartrain

Bibliothèque Mazarine, Paris, "Nation Iroquoise," manuscrit 1964

National Archives of Canada (NAC), Ottawa, "Nation Iroquoise," Manuscript Group 7, IV, vol. 1964

Printed Sources

Anonymous. "Memoire sur les coutumes et usages des cinq nations iroquoises du Canada." In *Variétés litteraires ou recueil de pièces, tant originales que traduites, concernant la philosophie, la littérature et les arts*, ed. J.-P. Baptiste and F. Arnaud. 4 vols. Paris, 1804. Reprint, Geneva: Slatkine, 1969.

Aumont, Gérard, co-ord. *Les prêtres de Saint-Sulpice au Canada: Grandes figures de leur histoire*. Sainte-Foy QC: Les Presses de l'Université Laval, 1992.

Axtell, James. *The Invasion Within: The Contest of Cultures in Colonial North America*. New York: Oxford University Press, 1985.

Bartram, John. *Observations on the Inhabitants, Climate, Soil, Rivers, Productions, and other matters worthy of Notice Made by Mr. John Bartram In his Travels From Pensilvania to Onondago, Oswega, and the Lake Ontario In Canada*. London, 1751. Reprinted in *A Journey from Pennsylvania to Onondaga in 1743 by John Bartram, Lewis Evans, and Conrad Weiser*. Barre MA: Imprint Society, 1973.

Baugy, Louis Henri, dit Chevalier de. *Journal d'une expédition contre le Iroquois en 1687*. Paris: Ernest Leroux, 1883.

Belmont Vachon, François de. *Histoire du Canada, [1608–1700].* Quebec: Société Littéraire et Historique du Quebec, 1840.

Bertrand, Albert Louis. *Bibliothèque sulpicienne, ou Histoire littéraire de la Compagnie de Saint-Sulpice.* 3 vols. Paris: Alphonse Picard, 1900.

———, ed. *Correspondance de M. Louis Tronson, troisième supérior de la Compagnie St. Sulpice.* 3 vols. Paris, 1904.

Boisvert, Aurélien, ed. *Nation Iroquoise.* Montreal: Éditions 101, 1996.

Boucher, Pierre. *Histoire véritable et naturelle des moeurs et productions du pays de la Nouvelle France, vulgairement dite le Canada.* Paris, 1664. Facsimile reprint, Boucherville QC: Société Historique de Boucherville, 1964.

Brandão, J. A., and William A. Starna. "The Treaties of 1701: A Triumph of Iroquois Diplomacy." *Ethnohistory* 43, no. 2 (Spring 1996): 209–44.

Brandão, José António. *"Your fyre shall burn no more": Iroquois Policy toward New France and Its Native Allies to 1701.* Lincoln: University of Nebraska Press, 1997.

Brown, George, et al., eds. *The Dictionary of Canadian Biography.* 14 vols. to date. Toronto: University of Toronto Press, 1966–.

Campeau, Lucien, S.J., ed. *Monumenta Novae Franciae.* 7 vols. to date. Roma: Monumenta Historica Societatus Iseu; Quebec: Les Presses de L'Université Laval, 1967–.

Codignola, Luca. "The Battle Is Over: Campeau's *Monumenta* vs. Thwaite's *Jesuit Relations*, 1602–1650." In *Missionaries, Native Americans, and Cultural Processes*, ed. Sylvia S. Kasprycki. Special issue. *European Review of Native American Studies* 10, no. 2 (1996): 3–10.

———. "Competing Networks: Roman Catholic Ecclesiastics in French North America, 1610–58." *Canadian Historical Review* 80, no. 4 (Dec. 1999): 539–84.

Deer, A. B. "La 'loi des condoléance' et la structure de la Ligue: Commentaire sur *The Great Law and the Longhouse: A Political History of the Iroquois Confederacy* par William A. Fenton." *Recherches amérindiennes au québec* 29, no. 2 (1999): 63–76.

Delanglez, Jean, S.J. *Frontenac and the Jesuits.* Chicago: Institute of Jesuit History, 1939.

Desrosiers, Léo-Paul. *Iroquoisie, 1534–1645.* Tome 1. Montreal: Études de l'Institute d'Histoire de l'Amerique française, 1947.

Dickinson, John A. "La guerre iroquoise et la mortalité en nouvelle-france, 1608–1666." *Revue d'histoire de l'Amérique française* 36, no. 1 (juin 1982): 31–54.

Dictionnaire historique de la langue française. 3 vols. Paris: Le Robert, 1992.

Dictionnaire historique du français québecois. Laval QC: Les Presses de l'Université Laval, 1998.

Dollier de Casson, François. *A History of Montreal, 1640–1672.* Ed. and trans. Ralph Flenley. London and Toronto: J. M. Dent, 1928. Originally published as *Histoire du Montréal.*

Eccles, W. J. *The French in North America, 1500–1783.* Markham ON: Fitzhenry and Whiteside, 1998.

———. "The Social, Economic, and Political Significance of the Military Establishment in New France." *Canadian Historical Review* 52, no. 1 (March 1971): 1–22.

Faillon, Étienne-Michel. *Histoire de la colonie française en Canada, [1534–1682].* 3 tomes. Villemarie: Bibilothèque Paroissiale, 1865–1866.

Faral, E. *Les jongleurs en France au moyen âge.* 2nd. ed. Paris, 1971.

Fenton, William N. *The Great Law and the Longhouse: A Political History of the Iroquois Confederacy.* Norman: University of Oklahoma Press, 1998.

———. "Northern Iroquoian Culture Patterns." In *Handbook of North American Indians,* ed. B. G. Trigger, 296–321. *Vol. 15: The Northeast.* Washington DC: Smithsonian Institution, 1978.

[de Galinée, René Bréhant]. "Ce que s'est passé de plus remarquable dans le voyage de M. M. Dollier et Galinée (1669–1670)." Ed. James H. Coyne. Ontario Historical Society Papers and Records, vol. 4. Toronto: Ontario Historical Society, 1903.

[Gélinas, Claude and Roland Viau], comps. "Nation Iroquoise." *Recherches amérindiennes au québec* 26, no. 2 (1996): 31–36.

Goddard, Peter A. "The Devil in New France: Jesuit Demonology, 1611–50." *Canadian Historical Review* 78, no. 1 (March 1997): 40–62.

Grand Larouse de la langue française. 6 vols. Paris: Librarie Larouse, 1973.

Greer, Allan. *The People of New France.* Toronto: University of Toronto Press, 1997.

Grimm, Jacob, and Wilhelm Grimm. *Deutsches wörterbuch.* Leipzig: Verlag von S. Hirzel, 1922.

Groulx, Lionel. *Histoire du Canada français*. 2 tomes. Montreal: Fides, 1976.

[Guyart, Marie]. *Marie de L'Incarnation, Ursuline (1599–1672), Correspondance*. Ed. Guy Oury. Solesmes, France: Abbaye Saint-Pierre de Solesmes, 1971.

Hatzfeld, Adolphe, et al. *Dictionnaire gênéral de la langue française du commencement du xviie siècle jusqu'a nos jours*. 2 vols. Paris: Librarie Delagarve, 1926.

Heidenreich, Conrad. "Early French Exploration in the North American Interior." In *North American Exploration*, ed. John Logan Allen. Vol. 2: *A Continent Defined*. Lincoln: University of Nebraska Press, 1997.

———. *Huronia: A History and Geography of the Huron Indians, 1600–1650*. Toronto: McClelland and Stewart, 1971.

Hodgen, Margaret T. *Early Anthropology in the Sixteenth and Seventeenth Centuries*. Philadelphia: University of Pennsylvania Press, 1964.

Huguet, Edmond. *Dictionnaire de la langue française du seizème siècle*. 7 vols. Paris: Didier, 1954.

Jaenen, Cornelius. *The Role of the Church in New France*. Toronto: McGraw-Hill Ryerson, 1976.

Jamet, A., ed. *Les annales de l'Hotel-Dieu de Quebec*. Quebec, 1939.

Jennings, Francis, ed. *The History and Culture of Iroquois Diplomacy*. Syracuse: Syracuse University Press, 1985.

Kinietz, W. Vernon. *The Indians of the Western Great Lakes, 1615–1760*. Ann Arbor: University of Michigan Press, 1940.

Knowles, Nathaniel. "The Torture of Captives by the Indians of Eastern North America." *American Philosophical Society Proceedings* 82 (March 1940): 151–225.

Lafitau, Joseph-François. *Customs of the American Indians Compared with the Customs of Primitive Times*. Ed. W. N. Fenton. Trans. E. L. Moore. 2 vols. Champlain Society Publications, vols. 48 and 49. Toronto: Champlain Society, 1974 and 1977. Originally published as *Moeurs des Sauvages ameriquains comparée aux moeurs des premier temps*, 2 vols., 1727.

Lahontan, Louis-Armand, Baron de. *New Voyages to North America*. 2 vols. Ed. R. G. Thwaites. Chicago: A. C. McClurg, 1905.

La Potherie, Claude-Charles Le Roy de [dit Bacqueville de la Potherie]. *Histoire de l'Amerique septentrionale.* 4 vols. Paris, 1722.

Le Blant, R., and R. Baudry, eds. *Nouveau documents sur Champlain et son époque.* Vol. 1: *1560–1622.* Publication des Archives Publiques du Canada, no. 15. Ottawa: Archives Publiques du Canada, 1967.

Leland, Waldo. *Guide to Materials for American History in the Libraries and Archives of Paris.* Carnegie Institution of Washington, publication no. 392, vol. 1. Washington DC: Carnegie Institution of Washington, 1932.

Margry, Pierre, ed. *Découvertes et établissements des Français dans l'ouest et dans le sud de l'Amérique septentrionale, 1614–1754.* 6 vols. Paris: D. Jouaust, 1876–1886.

———. *Relations et mémoires inédits pour servir à l'histoire de la France dans les pays d'outremer.* Paris: Challamel Aimé, 1867.

Maurault, Olivier, P. S. S. *La Compagnie de Saint-Sulpice au Canada.* Montreal, 1957.

Migne, L'Abbé. *Oeuvres Complète de M. Tronson, Superieur de Séminaire de Saint-Sulpice Réunis pour la premiere fois en collection . . . .* 2 vols. Paris, 1857.

Moogk, Peter. *La Nouvelle France: The Making of French Canada—A Cultural History.* East Lansing: Michigan State University Press, 2000.

[Morin, Marie]. *Histoire simple et véritable.* Ed. Ghislaine Legendre. Montreal: Les Presses de L'Université de Montreal, 1979.

O'Callaghan, E. B., ed. *Documents Relative to the Colonial History of the State of New York.* 15 vols. Albany: Weed, Parsons, 1856–1883.

Page, Christopher. *The Owl and the Nightingale.* Berkeley: University of California Press, 1989.

Perrot, Nicholas. *Memoire sur les moeurs, coustumes et relligion des Sauvages de l'Amerique septentrionale.* Ed. R. P. J. Tailhan. Leipzig and Paris: Librarie A. Franck, 1864.

Peyser, Joseph L., trans. and ed. *On the Eve of the Conquest: The Chevalier de Raymond's Critique of New France in 1754.* East Lansing: Michigan State University Press, 1997.

Preston, Richard, and Leopold Lamontagne. *Royal Fort Frontenac.* Toronto: Champlain Society, 1958.

[Radisson, Pierre Esprit]. *The Explorations of Pierre Esprit Radisson.* Ed. Arthur T. Adams. Minnesota: Ross and Haines, 1961.

Rapporte de l'archiviste de la province de Quebec.

[Raudot, Antoine]. *Relation par lettres de l'Amerique septentrionale.* Ed. Camille de Rochemontiex. Paris: Letouzey et Ané, 1904.

Richter, Daniel K. "Ordeals of the Longhouse: The Five Nations in Early American History." In *Beyond the Covenant Chain: The Iroquois and Their Neighbors in Indian North America, 1600–1800*, ed. Daniel K. Richter and James Merrell. Syracuse: Syracuse University Press, 1987.

Rochemonteix, Camille de, ed. Introduction. *Relation par lettres de l'Amerique septentrionale.* Paris: Letouzey et Ané, 1904.

Roy, Pierre-Georges. *La famille de La Porte de Louvigny.* Lévis QC, 1939.

Sagard, Gabriel. *Histoire du Canada.* Paris, 1636.

——. *The Long Journey to the Country of the Hurons.* Ed. G. M. Wrong. Trans. H. H. Langton. Champlain Society Publications, vol. 25. Toronto: Champlain Society, 1939.

Sayre, Gordon. *Les Sauvages Américains: Representations of Native Americans in French and English Colonial Literature.* Chapel Hill: University of North Carolina Press, 1997.

Silvy, Antoine. *Letters from North America.* Trans. Ivy Alice Dickson. Belleville ON: Mika, 1980.

Snow, Dean. *The Iroquois.* Cambridge: Blackwell, 1994.

Starna, William A., and J. A. Brandão. "From the Mohawk-Mahican War to the Beaver Wars: Questioning the Pattern." *Ethnohistory* (forthcoming).

Starna, William A., and John H. Relethford. "Deer Densities and Population Dynamics: A Cautionary Note." *American Antiquity* 50, no. 4 (1985): 825–32.

Starna, William A., and R. Watkins. "Northern Iroquoian Slavery." *Ethnohistory* 38, no. 1 (Winter 1991): 34–57.

Starna, William A., et al. "Northern Iroquoian Horticulture and Insect Infestation: A Cause for Village Removal." *Ethnohistory* 31, no. 3 (Summer 1984): 197–207.

Thwaites, R. G., ed. *The Jesuit Relations and Allied Documents, 1610–1791.* 73 vols. Cleveland: Burrows Bros., 1896–1901.

Trelease, Allen. *Indian Affairs in Colonial New York*. Ithaca: Cornell University Press, 1960.

Trésor de la langue française: Dictionnaire de la langue française du xix et du xx siècle. 16 vols. Paris: Centre National de la Recherche Scientifique, 1994.

Trigger, B. G., ed. *Handbook of North American Indians*. Vol. 15: *The Northeast*. Washington DC: Smithsonian Institution, 1978.

Trudel, Marcel. *Le débuts du régime seigneurial*. Montreal: Éditions Fides, 1974.

Vachon, André. "Colliers et ceintures de porcelaine chez les indiens de la Nouvelle-France." *Le Cahiers des Dix* 35 (1970): 251–78.

———. "Colliers et ceintures de porcelaine dans la diplomatie indienne." *Le Cahiers des Dix* 36 (1971): 179–92.

Viau, Roland. *Enfants du néant et mangeurs d'âmes: Guerre, culture et société en Iroquoisie ancienne*. Montreal: Boréal, 1997.

Index

Page numbers in italics refer to illustrations.

In

THE IROQUOIANS AND THEIR WORLD

Nation Iroquoise: A Seventeenth-Century Ethnography of the Iroquois
by José António Brandão

"Your Fyre Shall Burn No More": Iroquois Policy toward New France and Its Native Allies to 1701
by José António Brandão

www.ingramcontent.com/pod-product-compliance
Lightning Source LLC
Chambersburg PA
CBHW020811300326
41914CB00075B/1683/J
9780803213234